T0302296

Economic Change and Wellbeing

Technological progress and globalization have generated indisputable benefits, but also relevant costs, such as growing economic inequality, economic fluctuations, and financial instability. Mainstream economics has usually considered these costs as temporary, evenly distributed, and more than compensated by the gains of the phases of economic expansion. In this book, which focuses mainly (though not only) on the labor market, the authors contend that the major costs of the intensified process of creative destruction, through which economic change proceeded, have been ignored and the benefits overrated, thus incorrectly estimating the net impact of economic growth on subjective wellbeing. The book argues that the positive consequences of economic change and globalization may not compensate for the negatives, because psychological losses are felt more strongly than gains (due to loss aversion) and the costs are unequally distributed (those on low incomes disproportionately suffer more). The result is an overall reduction in wellbeing and therefore appropriate policies are necessary to allow more people to enjoy the benefits of technological progress without suffering the costs. The authors develop a comprehensive framework in which the socio-psychological context and educational level of a community determine the most suitable policies both for the short and for the long run. The book makes an invaluable contribution to the literature on economic growth and development, labor economics, the economics of wellbeing, and applications of behavioral economics.

The readers that may be interested in this book are economists and other social scientists, but also general readers, since the analysis is maintained simple and accessible. University teachers can use the book for courses on economic growth and development, on labor economics, on the economics of human capital, on the economics of wellbeing, and on applications of behavioral economics.

Fabio D'Orlando is Associate Professor of Economics at the University of Cassino, Italy. His research interests are in behavioral economics, economics and psychology, technological unemployment, history of economic ideas, classical-type theory, European integration and crises.

Francesco Ferrante is Full Professor of Economics. Ferrante's recent research interests include the effects of university inputs and university organization on students' achievement and graduates employability; the impact of education and social programs on the labor market; labor market institutions and macroeconomic performance; education and subjective wellbeing; the role of education in entrepreneurship and growth.

Albertina Oliverio is Professor of Epistemology of Social Sciences at the University G. d'Annunzio of Chieti-Pescara, Italy and Professor of Methodology of Social Sciences at University Luiss G. Carli of Rome. Her research interests are in epistemology and methodology of social sciences; rationality and decision making; social processes, social norms and human action.

Routledge Frontiers of Political Economy

Markets in their Place
Context, Culture, Finance
Edited by Russell Prince, Matthew Henry, Carolyn Morris, Aisling Gallagher and Stephen FitzHerbert

China's Belt and Road Initiative
The Impact on Sub-regional Southeast Asia
Edited by Christian Ploberger, Soavapa Ngampamuan and Tao Song

Capital and Capitalism
Old Myths, New Futures
Rogene A. Buchholz

Economic Change and Wellbeing
The True Cost of Creative Destruction and Globalization
Fabio D'Orlando, Francesco Ferrante and Albertina Oliverio

Capitalism, Development and Empowerment of Labour
A Heterodox Political Economy
Hartmut Elsenhans

Financialisation in the Automotive Industry
Capital and Labour in Contemporary Society
Marcelo José do Carmo, Mário Sacomano Neto and Julio Cesar Donadone

Political Economy of Financialization in the United States
A Historical-Institutional Balance-Sheet Approach
Kurt Mettenheim

For more information about this series, please visit: www.routledge.com/
Routledge-Frontiers-of-Political-Economy/book-series/SE0345

Economic Change and Wellbeing

The True Cost of Creative Destruction and Globalization

Fabio D'Orlando, Francesco Ferrante and Albertina Oliverio

LONDON AND NEW YORK

First published 2022
by Routledge
2 Park Square, Milton Park, Abingdon, Oxon OX14 4RN

and by Routledge
605 Third Avenue, New York, NY 10158

Routledge is an imprint of the Taylor & Francis Group, an informa business

British Library Cataloguing-in-Publication Data
A catalogue record for this book is available from the British Library

Library of Congress Cataloging-in-Publication Data
A catalog record for this book has been requested

ISBN: 978-0-367-86298-5 (hbk)
ISBN: 978-1-032-06197-9 (pbk)
ISBN: 978-1-003-01823-0 (ebk)

DOI: 10.4324/9781003018230

Typeset in Times New Roman
by Apex CoVantage, LLC

Contents

5 Conclusions: looking for sustainable economic change 110

Illustrations

Figures

Tables

Introduction

In the last 40 years or so, technological change and globalization have greatly intensified the dynamics of the world economy, bringing about – among other things – a shorter knowledge life cycle. This acceleration has generated indisputable benefits, but also considerable costs, such as growing wage polarization and economic inequality, increasing temporary employment, the working poor, ever greater skill and educational mismatch, more frequent economic fluctuations, and greater financial instability. Mainstream economics,[1] based on maximizing behaviors of fully informed agents (or agents with rational expectations), has usually seen these costs as temporary, evenly distributed, and more than offset by the gains in the phases of economic expansion.

In this book, which focuses mainly (though not only) on the labor market, we contend that the major costs of the intensified process of creative destruction, through which economic change proceeded, have been ignored and the benefits overrated, thus incorrectly estimating the net impact of economic growth on subjective wellbeing. Among the main failures of the *rhetoric of economic growth without regret*, which inspired OECD policymaking over the last 40 years or so, there is a lack of recognition of a major feature of the human mind, *loss aversion*. The tendency towards asymmetric assessment of gains and losses should lead to a revision of the trade-off between economic growth and macroeconomic stability, which conventionally assigns to the former a very high priority in policymaking. Accordingly, we use insights from behavioral economics, happiness economics, and economics of human capital to evaluate the true impact of economic change and globalization on people's wellbeing. We maintain that the positive consequences may not compensate for the negative ones since it can easily happen that (a) the costs are greater than the gains – mainly due to loss aversion. (b) these costs are unequally distributed, and (c) they hit hardest the weakest subjects, i.e., those who suffer greater losses for a given reduction in income, with in turn reduction in the average aggregate wellbeing. We, therefore, argue that appropriate policies are necessary to enjoy the benefits of technological progress, i.e., to increase the social returns of creative destruction.

The key objects of our analysis are technological change and the linked concept of creative destruction, which represent the main engines of growth and the main causes of globalization. Indeed, at the end of the eighteenth century, the countries

DOI: 10.4324/9781003018230-1

that adopted appropriate pro-market institutions started to grow very fast and enjoyed the fruits of the diffusion of innovations through creative destruction. At the time, lacking labor market regulations and social protection, the process of economic change generated winners and losers among social groups and, generally speaking, a very unfair sharing out of the cake. At the end of the nineteenth century, fear of social unrest and an increased social awareness led many governments to adopt policies and create institutions to protect people from various social risks and redistribute the gains of innovation and economic change. Since then, the political climate around the world has been characterized by waves of regulation and deregulation. Periods of strong reliance on the virtues of unregulated markets have been followed, after major recessions, by recognition of the need to regulate, protect people, and redistribute the benefits of economic change. Things changed in the 1980s when, due also to the prevalence of free-market economic theorists and in particular of New-Classical Macroeconomists, the world economy, in general, saw a long period of progressive and increasing deregulation, and in the meanwhile technological change greatly intensified. As a consequence, in the face of increasing uncertainty, workers are now less protected and more insecure while the redistributive mechanisms are weaker than 40 years ago. Furthermore, growing inequality and reduced social mobility attest to the fact that expectations of upward social mobility that might have justified deregulation and lack of redistribution resulted in mere illusion for most people.

The notion that inspired deregulation is that the net benefits of innovation through creative destruction can be maximized under a free market regime with minimal public intervention. This argument is theoretically supported by models showing that the representative risk averse maximizing agent would benefit in terms of consumption stream from abstaining from regulating the economy, i.e., not imposing constraints that limit the markets' allocative efficiency.

We argue that the true costs of economic change borne by the workers and their families during downturns are much more severe than expected, include significant nonpecuniary and psychological components, and are unevenly distributed among individuals holding different levels of human capital, i.e., they are more severe for the less-skilled workers. On the basis of the insights provided by behavioral economics, we critically assess this point in the context of the faster obsolescence of human capital brought about by the intensified dynamics of economic change. We argue that, even if income losses and gains cancel each other out during an entire business cycle, the average aggregate wellbeing losses are greater than the wellbeing gains. It goes without saying that our conclusions apply even more during recessions.

Our aim is not only to reassess the cost of economic change brought about by faster innovation dynamics. We also argue that, due to prevailing cannibalization among new products and scant innovative content of a large proportion of them, the benefits of innovation are lower than generally claimed.

Where do we go from here? Is it feasible to govern creative destruction and economic change so that it becomes a win-win strategy? We maintain that a fine-tuned mix of macroregulation and microregulation policies, relying more on the latter than on the former, can do the job. The overall aim of this integrated policy package is to increase the social returns of creative destruction. First, we should go back to the old idea that macrostabilization policies are needed to reduce economic fluctuations and uncertainty in the system. Second, inclusive and well-designed education and training policy should be targeted to enhancing people's adaptability and employability within a life cycle perspective. Third, labor market policy should accompany workers along the process of creative destruction through measures including job protection, unemployment benefits, and lifelong learning programs. Fourth, active industrial and technology policies should be implemented to (a) redirect technical change in socially and environmentally sound ways, (b) help economically viable businesses to address situations of financial fragility, and (c) facilitate the process of reallocation of workers from less efficient firms and industries to more efficient ones. Finally, the allocation of public funds to privately or publicly managed projects should be assessed through appropriate metrics of the social returns of these projects. This integrated policy package should be designed to minimize its burden on markets.

However, we also maintain that there is no *one size fits all* policy approach. A comprehensive and eclectic policy package will thus encompass policies that range from mainstream (for example, in countries with a highly educated workforce) to Keynesian (for example, in countries with a poorly educated workforce), depending upon the characteristics of the community to which it is addressed. The key element which links together apparently different policies, giving them intrinsic coherence, is mainly the extent to which they suit a society's culture and people's endowment of human capital. The ample role assigned, in this context, to governments should be complemented by greater accountability of politicians and public action: market and nonmarket failures are equally deleterious for a society's welfare.

The book is organized as follows.

In Chapter 1 we discuss the causes (separately considering shocks and policies) and the main consequences (in particular for the labor market) of economic change. In Chapter 2 we focus on mainstream economic analysis, describing the theoretical approaches through which the orthodox economists arrived at the notion of the welfare-enhancing nature of technological progress boosted by market liberalization. In Chapter 3, after a brief general assessment of the main weaknesses of the traditional approach, we propose a thorough analysis of the true costs and benefits of economic change which reverses mainstream economic thinking by taking into full account its impact on people's wellbeing. In Chapter 4, we illustrate the integrated policy package that might be implemented to increase the social returns of creative destruction. Finally, Chapter 5 draws the main conclusions.

Note

1 In this book we refer to orthodox theories/mainstream economic theories/traditional economic theories/neoclassical economic analysis as the corpus of theories based on methodological individualism and the idea that markets work fairly well.

1 Causes and consequences of economic change

Over the last few decades, the world economy has witnessed radical changes, with waves of deregulation and the contemporaneous intensification of the process of technological change. Among the most visible signs of these changes, we find the increase in international trade, migrations, and capital movements among countries; the rise of multinational firms; the impressive growth of the emerging economies; the rapid spread of economic crises; the increase in the dimension and role of (global and) internal imbalances; the growing external (public and private) debt of the developed countries; the end of inflation; and the rebirth of deflationary tendencies. Globalization has been used as a broad term encompassing most of the elements listed earlier, even if not all of them can be considered closely linked to globalization. The COVID-19 pandemic impacted this evolving situation by increasing the speed of the change but not the direction it went in.

The evolution of the contemporary economy described earlier had serious negative consequences for people's wellbeing (with increasing inequality, reduction in upward social mobility, and increase in downward social mobility for certain social groups and certain countries), for the labor market (with increasing unemployment risk and wage polarization), for international trade and capital movements (with the recurrence of protectionism), for economic growth (with striking slowdowns in some highly developed countries), and for political relations (with the rise of populism). As a result, the balance between the costs and benefits of creative destruction, through which economic change proceeds, needs in our view to be carefully assessed to verify whether regulatory measures are required to reshape it.

The aim of this chapter is to illustrate the causes and major consequences of the processes described previously as a whole.

In particular, in Section 1.1, we offer a systematic analysis of the main causes of this evolution by dividing them into two categories: the causes that are independent of the conscious activity of the policymaker, such as technological progress (the ICT revolution and robotization), and the pandemic, and the causes that are a direct consequence of the conscious activity of the policymaker, such as market liberalization. We call the former shocks, the latter policies. Considered together, we maintain that these causes were the main drivers of the most recent phases of the process of globalization, discussed in Section 1.1.3.

DOI: 10.4324/9781003018230-2

In Section 1.2, we describe the consequences of both shocks and policies for the labor market, with an increase in temporary employment, reduction of the labor income share, deteriorating employment conditions for unskilled workers and workers performing routine and repetitive tasks, job and wage polarization, and increasing skill and educational mismatch.

Finally, in Section 1.3, we discuss some of the consequences of shocks and policies for the economy as a whole, with growing inequality, diverging trends in social mobility, and the rise of populism and protectionism.

1.1 Causes of economic change

As summarized earlier, the causes of economic change can be divided between shocks and policies. Let us start with the shocks.

1.1.1 Shocks: industrial revolutions (and the pandemic)

It is certainly true that economic policies, and in particular the modification of these policies which started in the 1980s, played a significant role in determining the current evolution of the world economy, but these policies would have been impossible, or would have resulted in different outcomes, without the rapid spread of technological innovation throughout the world.

In spite of the unanimous recognition of the crucial role played by technological progress, the period from the last two decades of the twentieth century to the first two decades of the twenty-first century often lacks adequate interpretation since scholars tend to confuse two rather different waves of technological progress: the third and the fourth industrial revolutions. This confusion results from a considerable degree of overlap between the two phenomena, since both occurred close in time and used similar technologies. But, albeit apparently similar, the last two industrial revolutions are in fact crucially different from one another and impacted economic reality in rather different ways.

It is no simple task to propose comprehensive labels and time spans for complex processes like industrial revolutions. In any case, the beginning of the first industrial revolution is conventionally placed in 1770 and was based on the development of the steam engine, whereas the beginning of the second industrial revolution is placed in 1870, and was based on the widespread development of electric power. During these revolutions, technological progress basically relocated workers from one sector (at first from agriculture, later from manufacturing) to another (in the beginning, to manufacturing, later to services) with a temporary increase in short-term unemployment but no notable impact on long-term unemployment. Furthermore, generally speaking, this displacement had a positive impact, at least in the longer term, on the income of the relocated workers.

The beginning of the third industrial revolution is usually placed in the 1970s and was characterized by the diffusion of the digitalization of information. The digitalization of information had a considerable impact on consumption behaviors and product innovation, with the invention of personal computers, cellular phones, digital cameras, etc. But it had the greatest impact on the industrial structure: productive processes became more flexible and required more skilled and fewer unskilled workers (and/or fewer workers performing routine tasks).

The consequences of the latter process can be, and indeed have been, interpreted in two different ways. Some scholars[1] refer to it as skill-biased technical change,[2] or skill-biased technological change, a process that caused a reduction in the demand for unskilled workers, which could easily be replaced by machines, and an increase in the demand for skilled workers, i.e., workers capable of using the new machines. As a consequence, the wages of unskilled workers fell while the wages of skilled workers rose, so that wage polarization and inequality also increased.[3] Other scholars[4] maintained that such an approach was unable to grasp some important empirical evidence, and focused instead on a slightly different scenario, which they called task-biased technical change or routine-replacing technical change. According to this latter interpretation, technological progress mainly impacted negatively on workers performing routine tasks by bringing their wages well below those of workers performing nonroutine tasks.[5]

It is worth noting that skill-biased technical change and routine-biased technical change are not simply different ways of interpreting the same phenomenon, but rather different phenomena that impact in different ways on the labor market. This is so since skill-biased technical change impacts positively on wages and income for higher-skilled workers, and so ameliorates the situation for countries with a higher share of skilled workers over the total workforce; symmetrically, it impacts negatively on wages and incomes for lower-skilled workers, and so worsens the situation for countries with a smaller share of skilled workers over the total workforce. Thus, this approach sees an increase not only in inequality between low- and high-skilled workers but also in the inequality between skilled countries and unskilled countries. On the contrary, task-biased technical change impacts on the single tasks of the production process, and in particular on routine tasks, that can more easily be carried out by machines or computers (software programs) independently of whether the same tasks had previously been carried out by low- or high-skilled workers. In this case, inequality will increase between workers performing different tasks and not between skilled and unskilled workers or countries: technological progress hits workers performing a single task within a given category of workers, e.g., bank tellers, but not workers performing a different task within the same category of workers, e.g., bank clerks. Furthermore, it can no longer be said that skilled workers and countries can avoid the negative impact of technological progress while unskilled workers and countries cannot: acquiring skills by investing in human capital might therefore not be a solution.

For the cases of both skill-biased and task-biased technical change, the general idea, supported by many empirical studies,[6] is that technological progress spreading from the third industrial revolution may have raised unemployment and lowered wages for unskilled workers and/or workers performing particular (generally routine) tasks, but has not increased long-term unemployment in general, since redundant workers have easily been reabsorbed in other jobs or tasks (albeit often with a lower wage or worse working conditions).

So, the third industrial revolution may have contributed, together with other causes (in particular, globalization and markets liberalization), to wage polarization and to increase in inequality (between workers and countries), but not to increase in unemployment. We will describe the consequences of technological progress for the labor market in greater detail in Section 1.2.

Apart from the impact on the labor market, the third industrial revolution also had a significant impact on other economic phenomena, most of which linked to the globalization process. In particular, thanks to ICT technological progress it became possible to move financial capital from one country to another almost instantaneously, to implement just-in-time production, to develop new financial instruments, and to coordinate and facilitate the management of multinational companies operating over different countries (thus opening the way beyond Coase's idea that there is a bureaucratic limit to the size of a firm). All these are characteristics of globalization, which we discuss in Section 1.1.3.

However, the ICT revolution also made room for another, more recent, industrial revolution, the fourth industrial revolution (Schwab 2016). At the center of this new wave of technological progress is, again, the development of ICT (in this case in the form of artificial intelligence) and the entry of robots endowed with artificial intelligence into the productive process. Robots and artificial intelligence change everything, and in particular change the impact of the new technologies on wages, employment, and the labor market.

A number of different definitions of artificial intelligence can be found in the theoretical literature (see, e.g., Wang 2008). According to Minsky (1968, p. v), artificial intelligence is "the science of making machines do things that would require intelligence if done by men. It requires high-level mental processes such as: perceptual learning, memory and critical thinking." For the limited purposes of this book, we will define artificial intelligence as the capacity of computer systems to follow a principle of rationality and reasoning similar to that followed by the human mind. Whereas, according to Freeman (2015, p. 2):

> [t]he term "robots" refers broadly to any sort of machinery, from computer to artificial intelligence programs, that provides a good substitute for work currently performed by humans (. . .) it does not matter whether a robot/machinery has a humanoid appearance, as long as it can perform human functions.

In what follows we will refer mainly to robots endowed with artificial intelligence as the key feature of the new process, but more in general our argument holds for the introduction into the productive process of machines endowed with artificial intelligence.

The crucial difference between the third and the fourth industrial revolutions is that, once artificial intelligence comes on the scene, the possibility exists that robots may replace humans in all tasks and in all jobs, irrespectively of whether these tasks and jobs are routine or nonroutine, and irrespective of whether they are performed by skilled or unskilled workers: doctors, truck drivers, accountants, bank tellers, bank clerks, teachers, etc. – all these jobs and tasks can potentially be carried out by machines.[7] The problem of technological unemployment thus finds a place at the center of theoretical interest.

It is certainly true that the whole process of substitution of robots for human beings is only in its preliminary phases, and many economists are skeptical of the possibility that this might ever give rise to a mass unemployment scenario. In particular, even if scholars studying this phenomenon from a viewpoint other than that of the economists, such as social scientists or computer analysts (see, e.g., Brynjolfsson and McAfee 2011, 2014; Ford 2015), maintain that the introduction of robots (and artificial intelligence) into the productive process might actually result in mass unemployment (or even full unemployment, with the substitution of robots for human workers in almost all productive tasks), economists tend to deny that such a mass substitution is actually possible. We will discuss the reasons for the economists' skepticism about the possibility of technological (full) unemployment more thoroughly in the next chapter (Section 2.3.1). However, here we can anticipate the conclusion of our discussion with the observation that the problem appears to be a concrete factor in the future evolution of economic systems, as well as policy design.

A different phenomenon linked with technological unemployment is the increasing speed of skill obsolescence. Nowadays technological progress can be faster than the process of adaptation of human capital through formal education and training, so that the risk exists of people investing in a specific form of human capital which would have been profitable when the process of education began, but which turns out to be far less profitable, or totally out of date, when the process is completed. In other words, if formal education takes longer than skill obsolescence, education will never be able to match the skills required by the market. The result is structural unemployment due to persistent educational and skill mismatches. This implies that school and university curricula have to be changed, making people more adaptable, also through lifelong learning, or alternatively, that technological progress has to be slowed down. It is possible that neither of the solutions will prove feasible, so that other, more "creative" policies may be required.

Leaving aside structural unemployment, the progressive diffusion of technologies and business models based on AI is in any case increasing the unemployment risks for all.

Finally, another shock that hit the world economy, showing significant similarities with the phenomena described earlier, is the COVID-19 pandemic. At the outset, the consensus view described the economic consequences of the virus as a supply shock (see, e.g., Brinca, Duarte and Faria-e-Castro 2020; Papanikolaou and Schmidt 2020) with the direct impact of the pandemic on the economy lying in the fact that sick people, like the dead and people in quarantine, cannot work, thereby reducing employment and aggregate supply. And then there are the indirect consequences deriving from public policies designed to contain the pandemic, since extended lockdowns again reduce aggregate supply by preventing people from working even if they are not ill, dead, or in quarantine. These negative supply shocks appear all the stronger if we consider that national lockdowns not synchronized together jeopardize the functioning of global value chains as long as even only one single link in the chain, i.e., a single country, is interrupted (for example, because of a lockdown).[8] However, a new consensus view emerged when it became evident that the pandemic sharply increased uncertainty and so reduced the propensity to invest and consume, while consumption also fell because of the reduction of disposable income due to the shedding of workers, generating a demand shock (see, e.g., Guerrieri et al. 2020). Finally, some scholars (see, e.g., Fornaro and Wolf 2020) link the two shocks and theorize the possibility that the virus generated a doom-loop of aggregate demand and aggregate supply reinforcing each other.

Apart from the peculiar characteristics of the COVID-19 crisis, a point worth stressing here is that the pandemic sped up a couple of processes that had already begun to spread in the contemporary world: (i) growing popular opposition to globalization, mainly at the level of opposition to the movement of people from country to country (in the case of the pandemic since moving people are seen as plague-spreaders); (ii) the increasingly widespread use of new technologies, such as video conferencing and smart working, of new habits of consumption, such as shopping from home and food delivery, and the crowding out of obsolete activities, such as travel agencies and physical shops. Nothing new, but a further acceleration in the existing processes.

1.1.2 Policies

Economic policies, together with technological progress, played a central role in the transformations that have affected many economic systems over the last few decades. These policies have been particularly incisive and in general were based on the idea of reducing the role of governments in the economy, mainly by deregulating and liberalizing economic activities, together with privatizing public enterprises in countries where public ownership of the economic activities was pervasive. Such dynamics, albeit showing different features and timing in different countries and different institutional contexts, had common causes and was implemented through fairly similar policies worldwide.

The origins of this liberalist strategy are certainly to be found in economic and historical/political contingencies, but the theoretical developments in economic science that spread in the 1980s also played a role, at least in furnishing possibly robust theoretical foundations for the new approach to economic (de)regulation.

The role played by economic and historical/political contingencies in forming the new approach has mainly to do with the recognition that the foregoing (Keynesian) strategy of public intervention in the economy came up against a number of problems, and that these problems got worse over time. In particular the limits of the intervention strategy can be summarized in six points: (i) the surprising ineffectiveness and inflationary consequences of Keynesian policies (which had so far been particularly effective in counteracting unemployment and boosting economic performance) during the first oil crisis, after the Yom-Kippur war (October 1973); (ii) the (consequent) abandonment of Keynesian policies when the second oil crisis hit the world economy (around 1979); (iii) the collapse of collectivized socialist economies, in the 1980s, which was interpreted as collapse of countries that had put too much reliance on public intervention in the economy; (iv) the poor economic performance of many less developed countries that had relied on industrial policies and import substitution industrialization strategies (with the aim of boosting their growth rates and accomplishing the transition to industry); (v) technological progress, which allowed for transition from market failure to competitive markets, a development mainly affecting many natural monopolies; and (vi) the poor performance, inefficiencies, bureaucratic problems, poor rates of innovation, shown by public-managed firms in non-collectivized (as well as collectivized) economies.

The aforementioned (empirical) contingencies appeared capable of confirming the theoretical conclusions arrived at by the new mainstream approaches in the two decades that preceded the 1980s. Of these theoretical contributions a central role was played, in chronological order, by: (i) Milton Friedman's Monetarism, which started with a great deal of skepticism about public expenditure and deficit spending but ended up by denying the long-run real effects of any public intervention in the economy, whether monetary or fiscal, and asserting its negative inflationary consequences; (ii) Arrow and Debreu's (1954) Intertemporal General Equilibrium model, which presented rigorous foundations for the Walrasian idea of the possible existence of a competitive equilibrium for every market and time; (iii) Buchanan and Tullock's (1962) Public Choice Theory, which extended the maximizing principle to the behaviors of the policymakers, suggesting that public policies might be implemented not in the interest of the community or of a country's economic efficiency, but on the contrary with the purpose of maximizing the politicians' revenues; (iv) Stigler's (1971) Regulatory Capture Theory, which came to similar conclusions by emphasizing the possibility that small and organized lobbies might "capture" the policymakers by forcing them to pursue interests that are not those of the community; (v) the criticism many scholars made of the traditional Neoclassical Syntheses (and, implicitly, Keynes's approach) that it was not adequately microfounded, i.e., not rigorously built on the basis of the (maximizing) behavior of single individuals and firms described by traditional (mainstream) microeconomics; (vi) Lucas and Sargent's 1970s New Classical Macroeconomics, which, building on the Intertemporal General Equilibrium Theory and the Monetarist school's conclusions, and adopting Muth's rational expectations hypotheses, came to the conclusion that unemployment was always and only voluntary and public policies, both monetary and fiscal, were ineffective in the long as well as short run.

Therefore, starting from the eighties a huge wave of deregulation and liberalization policies swept over (a large part of) the world. These policies were implemented at different speeds and depths in the different countries, but were all characterized by a couple of common microeconomic and macroeconomic prescriptions: from the microeconomic perspective, market deregulation; from the macroeconomic perspective, reduction in public expenditure.

Here we aim to discuss a small, but critical, subset of these policies: (i) deregulation policies affecting the (domestic) labor markets; (ii) deregulation policies affecting the (domestic) financial markets; (iii) deregulation policies affecting international trade; (iv) deregulation policies affecting international capital movements, in both financial and real terms; and (v) policies aiming at reducing public expenditure and public debt.

Broadly speaking, this approach to economic policy was popularized in 1989 under the heading of the *Washington Consensus* and from then on it conditioned the actions of governments and national and international agencies such as the World Bank (WB) and the International Monetary Fund (IMF). On this basis, the *conventional wisdom* which policymakers followed in the developed and developing countries was that *markets are good whereas governments are bad*. And this paradigm shift was not limited to economists and policymakers: a cultural transformation based on an individualistic rather than solidaristic view of social relationships swept through Western societies, which went along with this shift. The view was championed by UK Prime Minister Margaret Thatcher.

Policies aimed at liberalizing the labor market ranged from reducing unemployment benefits, with the aim of increasing labor supply and work effort, to enhancing labor market flexibility by limiting the job protection provided for by employment protection legislation, with the aim of boosting firms' efficiency and thus labor demand, allowing firms to adjust employment to their needs more smoothly. This latter point is also consistent with the "popular view" (Agell 1999, p. 143) holding that labor regulations produce higher unemployment. Although there is scant empirical proof,[9] a majority consensus seems to exist among economists that reducing labor market regulations increases the efficiency of the economy and, in turn, also growth, production, income, and employment. Furthermore, the approach is fully consistent with many traditional (classical and neoclassical) models dealing with the functioning of the labor market, taking it as a market rigidity, and in particular, the absence of downward wage flexibility, which prevents the system from reaching full employment. Curiously enough, this traditional view is (at least partially) also shared by many scholars that claim to be Keynesian: both the Neoclassical Synthesis approach (with the works of Nobel laureates like John Hicks and Franco Modigliani) and the more recent New Keynesian Macroeconomics approach (with the works of Nobel laureates like George Akerlof, Joseph Stiglitz, and Michael Spence) reach involuntary unemployment results, on the basis of the assumption that in the short run wages are inflexible. Apart from the fact that, in contrast with the Neoclassical Synthesis, downward wage rigidity is microfounded in New Keynesian Macroeconomics, and is therefore hard to eliminate with simple policy measures, the shared albeit implicit conclusion of these approaches seems to be that getting rid of wage rigidities would eliminate involuntary unemployment, whereas market regulations might generate rigidities that raise unemployment. However, such theoretical conclusions on the role of labor market regulation have been questioned in a number of recent contributions: according to D'Orlando and Ferrante (2009, p. 107), "[m]any economists now believe that regulating a competitive labor market through employment protection legislation has no effect on the average level of unemployment, although it increases the variability of employment and reduces the efficiency of the economy."[10] The issue is still highly controversial, and the empirical data seem only to offer support to the somewhat more modest conclusion that regulating the labor market generates lower inflow and outflow rates from unemployment.[11]

More intriguing are the deregulation policies affecting the domestic financial markets, which were particularly incisive in some countries, such as the United States, which saw a great increase in the number and kinds of financial institutions allowed to lend money. These policies were accompanied by the diffusion of new financial instruments, such as Asset-Backed Securities (ABS), Mortgage-Backed Securities (MBS), Collateralized Debt Obligations (CDO), and Credit Default Swaps (CDS), and in general had the aim – and obtained the result – of guaranteeing that the credit risk was shared out among many subjects, each of whom would be hit only lightly should the borrower go bankrupt. In this way, the financial market was supposed to wax extraordinarily strong and, apparently, become immune from financial crises. Banks and financial institutions other than banks (which constitute the "Shadow Bank System") could lend a greater amount of money with, apparently, no risk.[12] Foreseeably, the actual result was an increase in the amount of credit lent to the economy, allowing more people to access the financial market. The idea was that this in turn would boost investment, with entrepreneurs devoting their extra financial resources to setting up plants and organizing new productive capacity, thereby generating economic growth. An increase in aggregate demand, income, consumption, and employment would also be generated. In this case, too, the theoretical bases for removing financial markets regulations can be found in a number of works, not necessarily of strict mainstream observance. To mention but a few, we may recall the New Growth Models (e.g., Pagano 1993 model) that link the growth of an economy to the efficiency of its financial system. Or the Modigliani–Friedman approach (see, e.g., Modigliani and Brumberg 1954; Friedman 1957), according to which consumption depends upon permanent income and/or wealth[13] but, in periods when people see their incomes falling below their life average, consumption is contained by the limits the banks set to individuals' ability to borrow: suffice it to relax these limits and consumption rises, as well as aggregate demand, even if the permanent income remains unchanged. All these can justify relaxing financial market regulations.

Liberalization of international trade followed a quite different path, since its history goes back (at least) to the GATT 1947 Treaty, well before the 1990s. However, the process gained momentum with the Uruguay Round, which started in 1986 and led to the birth of the World Trade Organization (WTO) in 1995. The aim of this complex evolution of international trade institutions was the progressive suppression of trade barriers, mainly in the form of tariffs on goods in an initial (GATT) phase, and in the form of tariffs on trade in services and protection of intellectual property in a second (WTO) phase, with key emphasis on non-tariff barriers to trade, which were regulated by the 1995 TBT (Technical Barriers to Trade) and SPS (Sanitary and Phytosanitary Measures) agreements. The trade liberalization process originated from the idea that increasing international trade could boost income and growth in both the developed and less-developed countries. This idea also had robust theoretical bases in the traditional theory of international trade, from the classical theory of absolute advantages by Adam Smith to the Ricardian and neoclassical Heckscher–Ohlin comparative advantages approach. According to all these theories, international trade would allow countries to specialize in producing and exporting the goods in the production of which they have a comparative (or absolute, in Smith's approach) advantage, importing the others. In this way, these countries would be able to increase their consumption possibilities, obtaining in exchange for the goods they produce (and export) a greater amount of the goods they do not produce (and import) compared to the amount of goods they could produce at home. And, at least according to Ricardo and the mainstream economists, this is true of all the countries taking part in international trade, and not only the countries which have an absolute advantage in producing some goods, as in Smith's approach. Ultimately, this is the strongest theoretical basis for globalization (or at least for globalization in the sense of an increase in international trade): all the countries involved in international trade can raise their real income, their consumption and, ultimately, their wellbeing. So, the idea was that removing all obstacles to free trade would increase world wellbeing.

Liberalization of international capital movements started around 1974 in the USA, but quickly "spread to the rest of the developed world in the second half of the 1970s and through the 1980s, and was essentially completed by the early 1990s" (Ocampo 2015, p. 3). It consisted of a common set of policies that impacted two rather different phenomena: liberalization of the possibility of making financial investments (portfolio investment, i.e., buying/selling bonds or equities for speculative purposes) and liberalization of the possibility of making real investments (foreign direct investment, i.e., building plants or buying equities in other countries with the aim of controlling the productive activity). Generally speaking, the aim of this policy as a whole was to (i) allow (both high- and low-income) single countries to finance their investments so as to boost economic growth even if they did not possess enough savings, or did not want to reduce their consumption to raise savings, by using funds from abroad, and (ii) enjoy the economic spillovers of foreign direct investments, which proved to be effective in generating economic growth in many economies. Also, this approach is fully consistent with traditional theory. In particular, focusing only on some of the most important approaches, liberalizing capital movements to boost growth appears consistent with both the traditional mainstream approach to capital movement developed by Nobel laureate Robert Mundell in 1957 and with the more recent New Growth Theories developed, again in the 1980s, by many scholars and in particular by Nobel laureates Robert Lucas and Paul Romer. According to Mundell, in the presence of differences in capital endowments among countries, capital would move from the countries in which it was relatively abundant, and so less productive and less remunerated, to countries in which it was relatively scarce, and so more productive and more highly remunerated, allowing for better capital distribution and higher growth rates. And, consistently with New Growth Theories, when multinational firms localize (some phases of) their production processes in other countries, they not only raise the capital endowment of that country, its employment, its production, and its exports but also generate spill-overs, i.e., positive externalities. These spillovers consist in an increase in human capital (thanks to training for local workers hired by the firm), in knowledge capital (thanks to the possibility for local entrepreneurs to imitate the technologies used by the multinational firm), in the competitiveness of local firms (that can imitate the behavior of the multinational firm), etc. These spillovers correspond to the externalities that, according to the New Growth Theories, can boost growth: human capital and knowledge capital in particular.

Finally, in recent years, a key role has been played by policies aiming at reduc-ing public expenditure and public debt. The reduction of public expenditure and public debt, or at least reduction of the public debt/GDP ratio, was the main pro-posal of a number of theoretical contributions that found circulation after the 1970s and were built around a triple set of foundations: (i) the Ricardo–Barro argument, according to which raising the public debt will induce subjects to expect a rise in future taxation and hence a reduction in their permanent income, so that they will immediately reduce consumption and increase savings, bringing aggregate demand down and so counteracting the rise in aggregate demand generated by expansionary fiscal policies; (ii) the idea that raising the public debt will raise the interest rate due to a reduction of market confidence (or, in a more theoretical fashion, due to a rise in the demand for money caused by higher income), lower-ing investments, capital accumulation, and ultimately growth rates; and (iii) the controversial contributions by Reinhart and Rogoff (Reinhart and Rogoff 2010; Reinhart, Reinhart and Rogoff 2012) who find empirical evidence that raising the public debt lowers growth, indirectly confirming (ii). On these bases, a number of further politically influential contributions argued that reducing public interven-tion in the economy will lower the budget deficit (or even generate a surplus) and, with it, the rate of growth of the public debt (or even reduce public debt). The amelioration of public finances will increase market confidence and so bring the interest rates down; generate short downturns and raise unemployment, thereby bringing wages down; reduce expected future taxation (necessary to repay the public debt). As a result, investments will rise (due to lower interest rates, wages, and expected taxation on investment revenues) as well as consumption (due to lower expected taxation). Higher investments will boost growth, while higher consumption will guarantee recovery from the initial (short) downturn. These dynamics have been theorized, with small differences, by various scholars. In par-ticular, Alesina and Ardagna (2009) focused on investments, Giavazzi and Pagano (1990, 1996) on consumption.

1.1.3 Globalization

Both the shocks and the policies described in the previous two sections repre-sent some of the characteristic features, but to some extent also the causes, of globalization.

There are a number of definitions of "what globalization is." For the limited purposes of the present book, and focusing in particular on its more recent phases, we define globalization as a phenomenon characterized by "an increasing liberalization of restrictions on the mobility of goods, services, capital (both real and financial) and technological knowledge" (Gupta and Choudhry 1997, p. 1). The causes are to be found in "[t]he recent revolution in transport and information technologies [that] is acting as a great catalyst, accelerating the process to an often unmanageable extent for many developing countries" (Gupta and Choudhry 1997, p. 1).

More in general, from an economic viewpoint, and considering in particular (but not exclusively) the most recent phases of the process, globalization is characterized by growth in international trade and the share of international trade over world GDP; increase in the mobility (and speed of mobility) of capital and financial services among countries; a striking rise in foreign direct investments (FDI), offshoring processes, fragmentation of production and intra-firm trade, all elements connected with the way multinational firms are looming ever larger; an increase in outsourcing processes, with firms that now, thanks to technological progress, can more easily delegate a share of their production to other firms, domestic or in other countries (outsourcing, offshoring); faster circulation of knowledge and ideas among countries (driven by the movements of goods and capital, the spillover of foreign direct investments and the massive diffusion of the new media); and, finally, an upsurge in migrations and thus in the movement of labor from one country to another.

Figure 1.1 shows the trend in the globalization of economic activity in recent years with three indicators regarding (i) trade, (ii) foreign direct investments, and (iii) expansion of global value chains (Trade/GDP, FDI/GDP, GVC/Trade).

International migrations are another central element of the globalization process. In addition to wars and ethnic and religious conflicts, transformations in the global value chains have greatly affected emigration flows at the world level, between the developing and developed countries and within the group of developing countries. Between 1990 and 2019, the stock of migrants increased globally by 78% and by 83% towards developed countries. Figure 1.2 shows the trend in the stock of migrants by region of destination.

According to other estimates, international migrants, i.e., people living in a country other than their countries of birth, numbered 84 million in 1970, 90 million in 1975, 101 million in 1980, 113 million in 1985, 153 million in 1990, 161 million in 1995, 173 million in 2000, 191 million in 2005, 220 million in 2010, 248 million in 2015, and 272 million in 2019 (IOM 2020, p. 21).

Naturally enough, within the traditional approach migrations should play the same role played by capital movements: re-equilibrating the differences between different countries in the endowment of one of the factors of production, in this case, labor, as compared with the demand for it. The majority of (mainstream) theories on the topic (e.g., Corry 1996; Harris and Todaro 1970; Todaro 1976; Massey

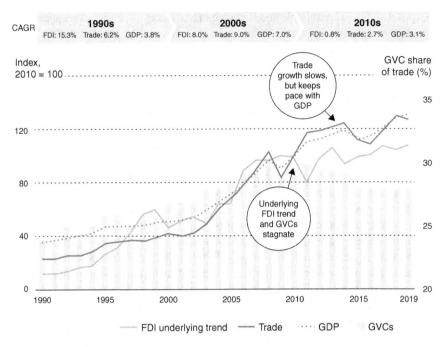

Figure 1.1 Trends in the globalization of economic activity, 1990–2019

Source: UNCTAD (2020)

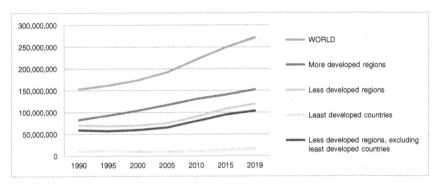

Figure 1.2 Stock of migrants by region of destination, 1990–2019

Source: UN database

et al. 1998), but also New Household Economics models (e.g., Stark and Bloom 1985; Fischer, Martin and Straubhaar 1997; Root and De Jong 1991), see the differences in wages as the main cause of international migrations: labor is seen to move from countries where it is relatively abundant, and so less productive and less remunerated, to countries where it is relatively scarce, and so more productive and better remunerated. In this way, not only will labor allocation improve, with the quantity of the factor rising where it is more needed and diminishing where it is less needed, but wages will tend to rise in countries where they were low, enhancing the workers' distributive share and reducing inequality (in wages) between countries. As usual, this is seen to favor economic growth.

From a less economic viewpoint, globalization has been characterized by the progressive diffusion of common ideas, habits, knowledge, market structures, economic policies, ideologies, and often laws and institutions, throughout the world. These latter characteristics explain why people often characterize globalization as "the global village" (and why, in some cases, they resist it).

With our experience of the coronavirus pandemic we now also know that another crucial characteristic of globalization, which was almost but not totally ignored by the standard definitions, is its capacity to guarantee rapid and global diffusion of pandemics. Furthermore, thanks to the interdependency of the economies, the impact of a pandemic on the world economy is nowadays definitely much greater than in the past.

Globalization is by no means new, and many scholars describe it as a phenomenon that started with the second industrial revolution. According to Baldwin (2006), globalization can be divided into two different phases, two different unbundlings. The first phase started around 1870, and was characterized by an increase in the movement of goods, and so in international trade, thanks to the falling costs and increasing speed of transportation, with inventions like the steam engine, steam trains, and railroads. Baldwin refers to this phase as the first unbundling – a phenomenon characterized by separation of the place where goods were produced from the place where they were sold and consumed. This first unbundling was interrupted with the First World War, in 1914, but regained momentum after the Second World War, around 1960, with inventions like cargo aircraft and containers. The first unbundling, again according to Baldwin, ended in 1995, but before it ended a second unbundling began, around 1985. This second unbundling was boosted by inventions like the digitalization of information, personal computing, and satellite communications, which brought down the costs and increased the speed of movement of ideas, information, and capital, resulting in the crucial process of fragmentation of production (i.e., the physical separation of the places of production), and hence in the development of multinational firms. So technological progress characterizes all the phases of the globalization process, but the ICT revolution characterizes its last phase, boosting it far beyond its past realizations.

A similar classification of the different phases of the globalization process was proposed by Krugman (2009). He distinguishes a first phase (until the First World War) characterized by the development of inter-industrial trade (countries specialized in different sectors trade with each other: for example, a country specialized in the production of corn exports corn to another country specialized in the production of cars, and the latter imports corn from and exports cars to the former); a second phase (after the Second World War) characterized by the development of intra-industrial trade (countries trade with one another even if they are specialized in the same sectors, the same industries: for example both countries are specialized in the production of cars, and both import and export cars); finally, the last phase, in recent decades, characterized by the fragmentation of production and intra-firm trade (different vertically integrated units of the same multinational firm, each specialized in a stage of the productive process, trade in intermediate goods from one country to another to complete the productive process: for example, a plant of a multinational in Korea builds the chassis of a car, and then sends it to another plant of the same firm in China where the productive process is completed).

In the following sections, we will discuss the direct and indirect consequences of the globalization process, focusing on not only its economic but also its social and political effects. We will start from the impact on the labor market. Here it is worth stressing that by reducing transportation costs for goods, services, and people, by reducing the costs and increasing speed for the movement of information, ideas, and capital, and by allowing for the treatment of great quantities of data in a short time, technological progress lies at the basis of the globalization process, together with the policy-driven reduction of trade barriers and hence, again, of trade costs.

1.2 Consequences for the labor market

The complex process of economic change described in the previous sections can also be interpreted with reference to the Schumpeterian concept of creative destruction. According to Schumpeter (Schumpeter 1976, p. 83), creative destruction is the "process of industrial mutation – if I may use that biological term – that incessantly revolutionizes the economic structure from within, incessantly destroying the old one, incessantly creating a new one." We might say that creative destruction and economic change are two faces of the same coin. We have described the main causes of the accelerated dynamics of change experienced by the world economy over the last 40 years, arguing that they pertain mainly to the technological and institutional spheres. Due to differences in the institutional arrangements and cultural factors, and in particular due to the differences in the rate and extent of deregulation and the resulting capability and propensity to govern it, the consequences of these dynamics in general and for the labor market, in particular, have differed in the different countries. Here a crucial role was played by measures implemented to redistribute the benefits of economic change and compensate and support the those losing out in the process. Within the OECD, countries with stronger welfare systems, stricter labor market regulations, and more unionized workers (i.e., European countries) have been able to control the side effects of creative destruction better, even if at the cost of slower economic growth.

1.2.1 *Temporary employment, labor income share, efficiency, and collective bargaining*

ICT-driven technical change and new external competition due to globalization brought about a loss of jobs in firms and sectors adversely affected. This process was coupled with downward pressure on wages for workers employed in sectors facing strong external competition and/or performing routine tasks more easily subject to automation. The consequences of these dynamics are not reflected in the unemployment rates so much as in the increase in temporary employment and the number of unemployment episodes in workers' lives, like the calm surface of an ocean hiding strong underlying currents due to thermal turbulence. Indeed, leaving aside the bulk of the great recession, data on unemployment rates in OECD countries have been fairly stable over the last 20 years: in 2000 the average unemployment rate was 6.2% and in 2018 it was even lower, standing at 5.3%. On observing unemployment rates by educational levels the picture does not change very much. On the other hand, it changes considerably on turning to temporary employment.

Figure 1.3 shows that between 1983 and 2019 the trend in the share of temporary labor contracts rose in both the OECD and Europe (16 countries), almost doubling in the latter.

Generally speaking, unemployment rates result from the combined effect of the number of unemployment episodes, i.e., frequency, and their spell, i.e., duration. For a given rate of unemployment, the two components are inversely related. Uncertainty and feelings of precariousness are generated more by the frequency of unemployment episodes than the spell (see chapter 3), especially if (a) the expected quality of jobs and wages decreases with the frequency of unemployment episodes and (b) unemployed workers are not provided with appropriate support through both active and passive labor market policy. But (a) and (b) are in fact the main outcomes of the process of regime switching described so far, which develops within a more flexible labor market characterized by more frequent unemployment episodes and shorter unemployment spells. The opposite holds

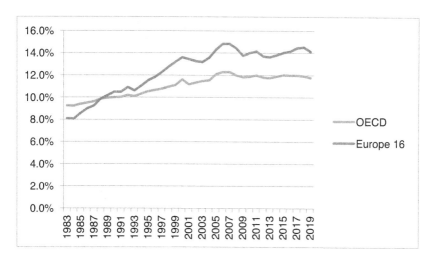

Figure 1.3 Share of temporary labor contracts, 1983–2019

Source: OECD online database

for a rigid labor market, e.g., due to strict employment protection legislation. The joint effect of the new policy regime and more rapid processes of creative destruction is that the labor market is more turbulent, with a higher share of temporary labor contracts and a higher frequency of unemployment episodes for the less-skilled workers. In Chapter 3, we discuss the implications of these circumstances for workers' wellbeing.

The process of economic restructuring has also been characterized by a shrinking share of value added and employment in the manufacturing sector in OECD countries and a redistribution of economic activities between territories, leading to a reshaping of the global value-added chains.[14] The dynamics of the labor income share in GDP is the main evidence of the consequences of the latter transformations: according to a reliable estimate, between 1980 and the 2000s for a selected group of G20 countries it fell by 0.3% per year (Figure 1.4):

> At least until the 1980s, a stable labor income share was accepted as a "stylized fact" of economic growth [. . .]. Over the past decades, however, this conventional wisdom has been challenged by the empirical evidence, which indicates a downward trend for the labor share in many of the countries for which data are available. [. . .] over the period from 1990 to 2009 the share of labor compensation in national income declined in 26 out of 30 advanced countries for which data were available, and calculated that the median (adjusted) labor share of national income across these countries fell from 66.1 per cent to 61.7 per cent. A more recent OECD calculation finds that the average adjusted labor share in G20 countries went down by about 0.3 percentage points per year between 1980 and the late 2000s.
>
> (OECD 2015, p. 2)

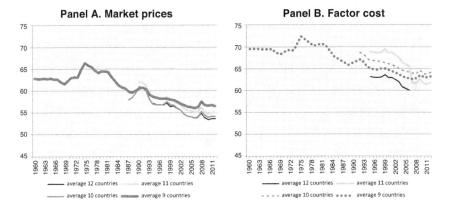

Figure 1.4 The adjusted labor income share at market price and factor cost in selected G20 countries and Spain

Source: OECD (2015)

Apart from the labor income share, liberalization and globalization also impacted the wages of low-skilled workers in a context of skill-biased technical change. Table 1.1 shows the cost of increasing real income through tariff reductions in terms of low-skill wage loss. According to these estimations, a fall in external tariffs of 10% brought about a 0.25% increase in real income and a 5.56% reduction in low-skill wages. Hardly a good deal for low-skilled workers.

In general, productivity gains have not been transferred to wages (Figure 1.5) and the gap between the two magnitudes increased over time, reaching around 20% in 2013.

Table 1.1 Distributive and efficiency consequences of trade liberalization: illustrative calculations

Initial tariff being removed	change in low-skill wages (A)	increase in real income of economy (AB)	absolute value of ratio (A)/(B)
40%	−19.44%	4.00%	4.9
30%	−15.22%	2.25%	6.8
20%	−10.61%	1.00%	10.6
10%	−5.56%	0.25%	22.2
5%	−2.85%	0.06%	45.5
3%	−1.72%	0.02%	76.6

Source: Rodrik (2018)

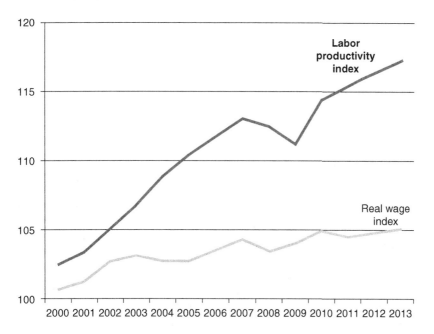

Figure 1.5 Trends in average wages and labor productivity in selected advanced G20 economies, 1999–2013

Source: OECD (2015)

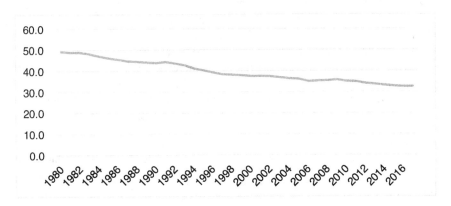

Figure 1.6 Union coverage 1980–2017.

Source: OECD database.

The change in the institutional regime also affected the role of collective bargaining. The generally declining bargaining power of the unions contributed to affecting the observed dynamics of wages. In Figure 1.6, we show the trend in average union coverage in the OECD, i.e., the share of workers covered by collective bargaining, which decreased steadily from almost 50% in 1980 to around 30% in 2017.

The new institutional and technological regime is responsible for drastic changes within the OECD, also among different groups of workers, leading to job and wage polarization.

1.2.2 Job and wage polarization

In Section 1.1, we showed that technical change and the diffusion of automation has brought about (and will probably continue doing so) skill and job polarization: routine tasks are progressively being taken over by machines and the number of tasks that can be automated is increasing thanks to the diffusion and development of AI. The jobs resisting automation, due to the limited applicability of new technologies, are the ones based either on manual nonroutine tasks or tasks requiring highly skilled workers who cannot be substituted by machines. This process has so far resulted in job and labor market polarization: employability appears to be U-shaped. A relatively small group of occupations, requiring low skills but characterized by non-routine tasks, and occupations requiring high skills in tasks that cannot be automated, show high employability. Conversely, a large share of the jobs in the middle of the skills distribution are facing decreasing employability and increasing unemployment risks. The main effect of such dynamics is downward pressure on wages for workers in the middle of the skill distribution characterized by routine tasks.

Another source of diverging trends in wages is the race between technology and education (Tinbergen 1974; Goldin and Katz 2009) resulting from skill-biased technical change. According to Autor, Goldin, and Katz (2020), this accounts for 75% of the increase in wage inequality in the USA between 1980 and 2000:

Educational wage gains and overall wage and income inequality have closely followed changes in educational attainment against a backdrop of increased relative demand for more-educated workers from skill-biased technological change (SBTC). The implicit framework is one of a race between education and technology (RBET). [. . .] The wage inequality increased at about the same rate from 1980 to 2000 as from 2000 to 2017. The variance of log hourly wages increased by 0.065 from 1980 to 2000 and by 0.058 from 2000 to 2017. But the college wage premium increased much more rapidly in the first period than in the second. The rise in the returns to college education explains a far larger share of the increased log hourly wage variance from 1980 to 2000 than it does from 2000 to 2017, accounting for 75 percent in the first period, but just 38 percent more recently.

(Autor, Goldin and Katz 2020, pp. 3 and 9)

The impact on wages of the dynamics of the labor market driven by the latter process in OECD countries is illustrated in Figure 1.7. It shows a fairly rapid increase in the wage premium enjoyed by the top 1% earners.

Therefore, the main legacy of the new institutional and technological regime has been increasing inequality among workers and, as we will see, diverging trends in social mobility in most developed countries.

1.2.3 Increasing skill and educational mismatches

ICT-driven technical change and the diffusion of AI are destroying jobs but, at the same time, might contribute to the creation of new occupational opportunities for workers in new sectors of the economy (World Bank 2019). Forecasts on the

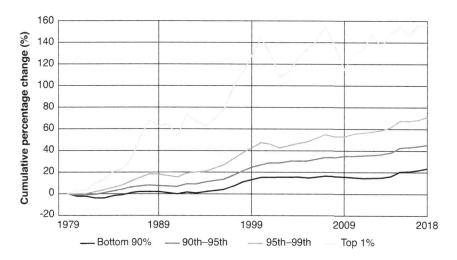

Figure 1.7 Cumulative percent change in real annual wages, by wage group, 1979–2018

Source: WEF (2020)

net effects of this process of creative destruction have yet to become sufficiently reliable. Independently of the future net effect, the rapid rate of change characterizing this process is bringing about a great deal of turbulence in the labor market, together with anticipated skill obsolescence, increasing labor market mismatches, and greater unemployment risks for a large share of the workforce that are not adequately captured by unemployment rates.

Indeed, skills and educational mismatches are another legacy of more intensive processes of creative destruction based on skill-biased technical change and a speedup in the race between education and technology. According to robust empirical evidence, they adversely affect productivity and also wages and workers' job satisfaction (e.g., Allen and van der Velden 2001; Ferrante, McGuinness and Sloane 2010).

In a static environment, matching between demand and supply of skills can be achieved and maintained quite easily. Conversely, educational institutions and workers have to fight hard to respond to rapid changes in labor demand if the environment is characterized by fast technological change. First of all, planning and implementing new educational curricula in response to signals coming from the labor market takes time and no coordination mechanisms exist to regulate the market for skills or avoid temporary excesses of supply and demand. An additional problem is that while educational choices are made early in life, their effects last forever and are based on limited information on future labor market prospects. Not surprisingly, they are a major source of regret in people's lives (Ferrante 2009).

Macroeconomic instability is another potential major source of educational and skill mismatches bearing long-term negative consequences. Negative macroeconomic shocks may exert permanent effects on young workers entering the labor market during downturns. There is strong evidence that mismatched young workers experience persistently worse employment conditions in terms of wages. In particular, the costs borne by young workers entering the labor markets for the first time can be very high even when they find a job. With bad labor market conditions skills matching will be less efficient and this initial poor-quality relationship between young workers and employers will produce long-lasting adverse effects on wages and career prospects. Some estimates for university graduates in the USA suggest that these effects may last up to 20 years and that they may imply a 20% total wage penalty compared with the luckier colleagues who entered in favorable times (Liu, Salvanes and Sorensen 2012; Oreopoulos, Wachter and Heisz 2012). This loss is regressive in that it has a greater effect on young workers from disadvantaged social backgrounds who cannot wait long for the right job and who cannot postpone labor market entry by investing in more education.

1.3 Other consequences

Apart from the consequences for the labor market, the process of creative destruction has impacted other aspects of the economy and society. In particular, in what follows we focus on increasing inequality, diverging trends in social mobility, and the spread of populism and protectionism.

1.3.1 Rising inequality and diverging trends in social mobility

The consequences of economic change for the workers and the general wellbeing depend not only on their wages but also on the availability of institutional arrangements to support those losing out and redistribute the gains of economic change. When wages fail to keep up with productivity increase, the main legacy of the deregulated process of innovation and globalization lies in greater inequality of income and wealth at the worldwide level and, specifically, in the OECD countries. In Section 1.2.1, we showed that the share of labor income has been greatly reduced in most countries over the last few decades. The opposite holds for the share of income accruing to the top earners: in the last 40 years or so, the share of income accruing to the top 10% and 1% of the income distribution increased everywhere (Figure 1.8–1.11). Economic growth brought about by economic change largely benefited the last two income groups whereas the bottom 50% of the income distribution received a tiny share of the cake. For some groups of workers, absolute levels of wages decreased between 1980 and 2019. The regime switching and the regressive distribution of the gains of economic change are also reflected in the trend in wealth distribution (Figure 1.12), which also appears to be cumulatively affected by the heterogeneity of returns on wealth favoring the top shares in wealth distribution.[15]

The aforementioned results also depend upon the ability of governments to undertake intervention programs designed to redistribute to the losers the gains obtained by the winners in the creative destruction processes. Actually, globalization and deregulation have seen the retreat of the State, complementing deregulation[16] and the global reduction in fiscal redistribution. This is all too evident in the data on the trend of the share of private versus public capital (Figure 1.13), entailing a weakened ability of the State to finance social insurance schemes and, more generally, mechanisms to compensate the "losers" and redistribute the benefits

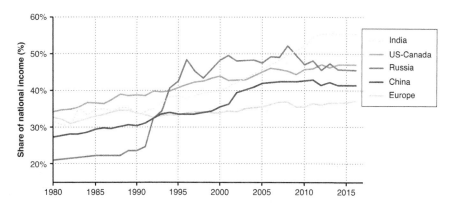

Figure 1.8 Top 10% income shares across the world, 1980–2016: rising inequality almost everywhere, but at different speeds

Source: WEF (2020)

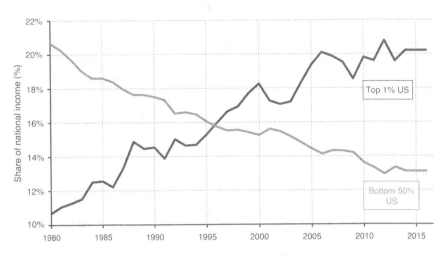

Figure 1.9 Top 1% versus bottom 50% national income shares in the USA and Western Europe, 1980–2016: diverging income inequality trajectories

Source: WEF (2020)

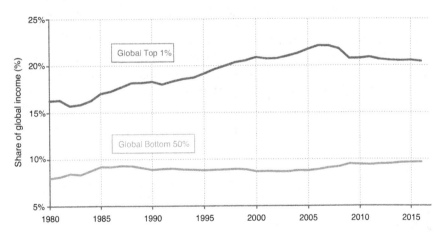

Figure 1.10 The rise of the global top 1% versus the stagnation of the global bottom 50%, 1980–2016.

Source: WEF (2020)

of creative destruction. This general trend is common to all OECD countries, independently of their institutional setting, and in particular of the redistributive orientation of their social and fiscal policy. Of course, national policy and institutions have shaped the process, and indeed the more redistributive systems are still more equal, e.g., the Scandinavian countries.

Inequality is a multidimensional phenomenon that should be assessed as such:

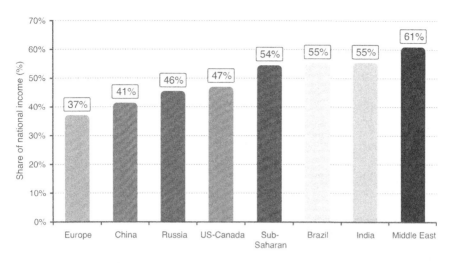

Figure 1.11 Top 10% national income share across the world, 2016

Source: WEF (2020)

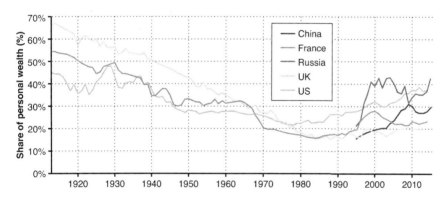

Figure 1.12 The rise and fall in personal wealth inequality (1913–2015). Top 1% share
of wealth

Source: WEF (2020)

Socio-economic status heavily influences employment prospects, job quality, health outcomes, education, and the other opportunities (including
access to the relevant networks) that matter to people's wellbeing. Children
whose parents did not complete secondary school have only a 15% chance
of making it to university compared to a 60% chance for their peers with
at least one parent who achieved tertiary-level education. Disadvantage at

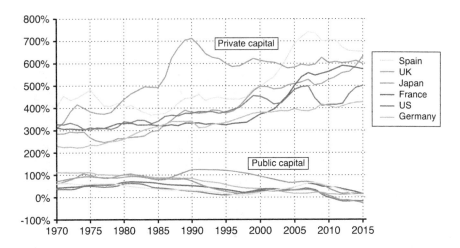

Figure 1.13 The rise of private capital and the fall of public capital in rich countries, 1970–2016

Source: WEF (2020)

the outset can follow children throughout their lives. Educational disadvantage typically means not only smaller salaries, but, most worryingly of all, shorter lives. A 25 year-old university-educated man can expect to live almost eight years longer than his lower-educated peer on average across OECD countries; the difference is 4.6 years for women. The vicious confluence of poor educational opportunities, low skills and limited employment prospects can trap people in situations where they are also are far more likely to be exposed to environmental hazards and violence. As a result of this multidimensional inequality, while some individuals, cities and regions thrive, others fall further behind.

(OECD 2018a, p. 5)

Inequality is also closely linked to social (im)mobility, and both with technological progress. The empirical data confirm that social mobility has seen a sharp drop over the last few decades:

We find that rates of absolute mobility have fallen from approximately 90% for children born in 1940 to 50% for children born in the 1980s. The result that absolute mobility has fallen sharply over the past half century is robust to the choice of price deflator, the definition of income, and accounting for taxes and transfers. In counterfactual simulations, we find that increasing GDP growth rates alone cannot restore absolute mobility to the rates experienced by children born in the 1940s. In contrast, changing the distribution of growth across income groups to the more equal distribution experienced by the 1940 birth cohort would reverse more than 70% of the decline in mobility. These results imply that reviving the 'American Dream' of high rates of absolute mobility would require economic growth that is spread more broadly across the income distribution.

(Chetty et al. 2017, p. 2)

The *Great Gatsby* curve offers a telling description of the consequences of an unregulated process of creative destruction on these elements. It shows a negative relationship between inequality and upward social mobility (Figure 1.14): less equal societies are also less mobile (Bukodi et al. 2015; Corak 2013). But why are more flexible societies, as in the USA and UK, based on soft regulation and lack of redistribution and social protection, both less equal and less mobile? One possible answer to these two questions lies in the "POUM hypothesis" (the prospect of upward mobility, Benabou and Ok 2001; see Chapter 2, Section 2.4.3). According to this hypothesis, the absence of redistributive mechanisms *today* should be seen as a good thing by people at the bottom of the distribution seeing that, thanks to a more dynamic economy, they will enjoy social mobility in the future. Unfortunately, the empirical evidence provided by the *Great Gatsby curve* does not bear out the existence of this trade-off between equality and social mobility in the developed countries; rather, it offers a picture where the less regulated countries are also the countries offering scant chances of improving one's socio-economic status.

Intergenerational mobility is not the only way to assess social mobility:

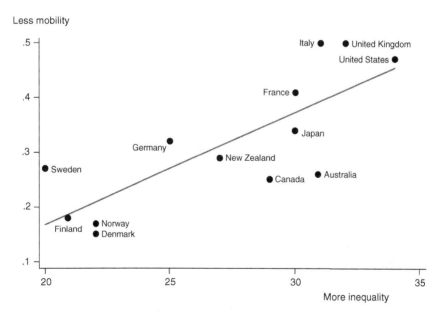

Figure 1.14 The *Great Gatsby* Curve

Source: Corak (2013)

Social mobility is a multi-faceted concept. For one thing, it can be under-stood as mobility between parents and children or grand-children – the so-called *inter-generational* mobility. Alternatively, the concept can encompass only personal life course perspectives – this is *intra-generational* mobility. [. . .] for most people the big picture across generations counts probably more when thinking about mobility than what happens over shorter time periods: when assessing their chances of mobility people tend to compare how they live at present times with how they grew up and how their parents lived.

(OECD 2018a, p. 13)

Unequal education opportunities, together with lack of access to lifelong learn-ing, are the main channel through which income inequality fosters social immo-bility. This is also due to the properties of the technology of skills formation[17] (Cunha and Heckman 2007) and to the complementarity between education and training (Brunello, Garibaldi and Wasmer 2007). Skill and job polarization have the consequence of making lack of access to education the main long-term driver of persistent inequality and lack of social mobility. This outcome is not only unfair but also inefficient due to its impact on the allocation of human capital and talent. Talented individuals from disadvantaged social backgrounds are not allowed to make the contribution to social progress they would, in fact, be capable of. According to some empirical studies, the welfare costs of such an inefficient allocation of talents are not negligible (WEF 2020).

A graphic description of the impact of global competition evokes the *sticky floors and ceilings* that it generates:

Income mobility is low at the bottom and at the top of income distribution and is higher for those living in the middle class. This not only translates into more opportunities for them compared with other groups, but also into greater risks to fall down the ladder following unexpected life events such that unemployment or divorce.

(OECD 2018a, p. 15)

Social mobility is affected by the interaction of various factors: wages, access to education, the redistributive orientation of institutions, technology, etc. The World Economic Forum computed a composite index of social mobility which takes into account the latter factors.[18] The country ranking based on this metric is shown in Table 1.2.

Interest in upward mobility should not lead us to underestimate the impor-tance for the wellbeing of downward social mobility[19]: the presence of loss aversion (see Chapter 3) entails that the welfare gains of those individuals[20] enjoying upward social mobility may not be sufficient to offset the welfare loss of individuals experiencing downward social mobility.[21] Moreover, the downward social mobility of parents may account for the lack of upward social mobility through its impact on education opportunities (Major and Machi 2019; Alm 2011).

Table 1.2 The global social mobility index (ranking, first 30 countries)

Rank	Country	Score
1	Denmark	85.2
2	Norway	83.6
3	Finland	83.6
4	Sweden	83.5
5	Iceland	82.7
6	Netherlands	82.4
7	Switzerland	82.1
8	Belgium	80.1
9	Austria	80.1
11	Germany	78.8
12	France	76.7
13	Slovenia	76.4
14	Canada	76.1
15	Japan	76.1
16	Australia	75.1
18	Ireland	75
19	Czech Republic	74.7
20	Singapore	74.6
21	United Kingdom	74.4
22	New Zealand	74.3
23	Estonia	73.5
24	Portugal	72
25	Korea. Rep.	71.4
26	Lithuania	70.5
27	United States	70.4
28	Spain	70
29	Cyprus	69.4
30	Poland	69.1

Source: WEF (2020)

1.3.2 The rise of populism and protectionism

Another crucial consequence of recent economic change is the rise of populism.

> Countries where people are more pessimistic about mobility prospects are often those where parental situations in terms of education or income are more strongly correlated with the situation of sons and daughters. Of course, perceptions and expectations about mobility are influenced by a range of country and individual specific factors, but these perceptions matter in themselves, as they have economic, social but also political consequences [. . .] There is evidence suggesting that prospects of upward mobility also have a positive influence on life satisfaction and wellbeing. Inversely, high risks of downward mobility and loss of social status tend to reduce life satisfaction and undermine individual self-esteem, social cohesion and people's feeling that their voice counts, particularly among middle- and lower-income people. This reduces trust in

the sociopolitical system with potential negative consequences on democratic participation. This also strengthens political extremisms or populism.

(OECD 2018a, p. 13)

Actually, the direct and indirect consequences of technological revolution, globalization, and deregulation on individual self-esteem, social cohesion, and life satisfaction were quite predictable, since the theoretical models were rather univocal in identifying winners and losers. Therefore, also the rise of populism is not at all a surprise.

Returning to the very foundations of the approaches discussing the trade aspect of globalization, we can recall Samuelson's (1948) Factor Price Equalization (FPE) theorem, built within the Heckscher–Ohlin approach. In Section 1.1.2 we showed that the Heckscher–Ohlin approach can be used to demonstrate that (albeit under some rigid assumptions) all the countries engaging in international trade raise their income. The FPE theorem, albeit again under rigid simplifying assumptions, concludes that thanks to the sole functioning of international trade in goods and even in the absence of factor mobility among countries, there is a tendency towards the equalization of factor prices among countries. Simplifying a little, the logic of the theorem can be summarized as follows: a country with a high share of unskilled workers (compared to capital and skilled workers) will face high supply and hence low wages for unskilled workers and will specialize in the production and exportation of goods whose production requires a greater percentage of this low-remunerated factor; on the contrary, a country with a high percentage of capital and skilled workers (compared to unskilled workers), will face a lower supply and hence higher wages for unskilled workers, and will specialize in the production and exportation of goods the production of which requires a higher percentage of skilled labor and of capital. As a result of productive specialization, the demand for unskilled labor in the first country will rise, raising the wages of unskilled workers, and reducing the gap with the (generally higher) remuneration of skilled workers and capital. By contrast, the demand for skilled labor and capital in the second country will rise, raising the wages of skilled workers and the remuneration of capital, and increasing the gap with the (generally lower) remuneration of unskilled workers. Inequality is reduced between countries and in low-wage countries, but increases in high-wage countries.

Yet the theorem holds true only under very specific and unrealistic assumptions (two countries, two goods . . .), although its logic remains. Furthermore, similar results are also obtained on considering other aspects of the mainstream approach.

Take, for example, migrations. As discussed in Section 1.1.3, according to the standard approach, wage differentials determine international migrations: workers will leave countries in which labor supply (generally, of unskilled workers) is relatively high, and hence productivity and wages relatively low, towards countries where labor supply is relatively low, and hence labor productivity and wages relatively high. In this way, labor supply falls and wages rise in the labor-abundant country, whereas labor supply rises and wages fall in the labor-scarce country. Inequality diminishes in the former countries, increases in the latter, and diminishes between countries.

Finally, consider capital movements. The traditional view, contested later by Lucas with his paradox, is rooted in the Robert Mundell 1957 approach. As we discussed in Section 1.1.2, according to Mundell, capital moves from countries where it is relatively abundant, and so show low productivity and earn low remuneration, to countries where it is relatively scarce, and so show high productivity and earn high remuneration. As a consequence, capital remuneration rises where it is low (thanks to the reduction in supply caused by the outflow) and falls where it is high (thanks to the increase in supply caused by the inflow) with two crucial consequences: (i) the movement of capital, in particular in the form of foreign direct investment, from capital-abundant to capital-scarce countries, allows the latter to receive from abroad the resources they do not possess and thus to realize investments and boost growth; (ii) inequality between countries, in terms of both relative capital endowment (and capital remuneration) and growth rates, diminishes. Furthermore, in the case of the fragmentation of the productive process that characterizes the second unbundling of globalization, the fact that the fraction of the productive process localized abroad is often the one highly intensive in unskilled labor implies that by delocalizing production firms reduce labor demand, employment and wages for unskilled workers in the origin country of the foreign direct investment and raise labor demand, employment and wages for unskilled workers in the destination country. As a result, inequality rises in the origin (capital abundant) country and diminishes in the destination (capital scarce) country, while inequality diminishes between countries.

It is worth noting that different ideas on the theoretical causes of inequality do, in fact, exist. For example, according to Aghion, Caroli and Garcìa-Peñalosa 1999, the main source of inequality is not to be found in the globalization process, or in the increase in international trade, nor indeed in economic growth or organizational change, but in technological progress, which stimulates economic growth and increases wage inequality due to skill-biased technological change.

In any case, all these factors imply that traditional economic theory has a number of insights suggesting that income inequality between unskilled and skilled workers (and capital) will increase in high-income countries abundant in capital and skilled labor with a low unskilled labor supply, since in these countries the wages for unskilled workers will fall and the wages for skilled workers will rise; the opposite will happen in low-income countries relatively abundant in unskilled labor and scarce in capital and skilled labor, since in these latter countries the wages for unskilled workers will rise and the wages for skilled workers will fall. In other words, the winners in the globalization process are likely to be the unskilled workers in the low-income countries while the losers are likely to be unskilled workers in high-income countries.

Notwithstanding these simple and univocal implications of the theory, at an early phase, when the empirical data did not seem to bear out these dynamics, economists (and media) all over the world discussed the negative effects that globalization might have on low-income countries. Now the picture is clearer: the predictions of the traditional theories were fairly accurate: losers can actually be found among the middle class and unskilled workers in the "rich" countries, whereas winners can be found among the unskilled workers in the "poor" countries – which, as a result, are now becoming less poor – and among the skilled workers and capital in the "rich" countries. This state of affairs confirms the widespread opinion that the spread of democracy, and with it free elections, in the developing countries boosts globalization, whereas free elections in the developed countries end up by thwarting globalization.

The aforementioned conclusions on inequality are captured by the famous "old" elephant graph by Milanovic (2012)[22] represented in Figure 1.15, where the data stop in 2008, and in its 2018 version, represented in Figure 1.16 (Alvaredo et al. 2017, p. 51): the richest gain, the poorest gain, and the middle-class workers in the West European countries and in the USA lose. It is hardly surprising that the losers call for protection, i.e., they call for populist measures that, they hope, might be able to protect them from the impact of globalization. In other words, the losers call for a halt to the globalization process. They are probably a minority in their own countries, but the Stigler (1971) approach showed how an organized minority share of a population can "capture" the government and impose the policies they call for on the entire community.

The aforementioned state of affairs can account for the rise of populist movements, leading to phenomena like Brexit and the election in some major Western countries of populist governments which have explicitly tried to put a stop to globalization. Indeed, globalization, deregulation, and technological progress are closely interlinked; in fact, we would argue that due to them and, more in general, to more intense economic change, people are now more exposed than in the past to bearing the cost of uncertainty about the various events that may affect the quality

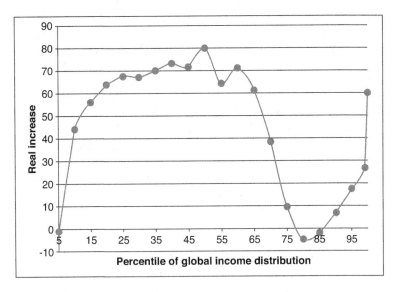

Figure 1.15 The elephant curve

Source: Milanovic (2012, p. 13)

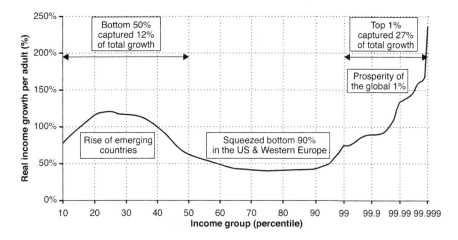

Figure 1.16 The elephant curve of global inequality and growth, 1980–2016

Source: Alvaredo et al. (2017, p. 51)

of their life (job loss, health conditions, crime, etc.; see, e.g., OECD 2018b). And the consequent rising perceived precariousness has adversely affected subjective measures of wellbeing (Clark and Oswald 1994; Clark, Georgellis and Sanfey 2001; Frey and Stutzer 2002; Clark et al. 2004; see Chapter 3), as also the rapid increase in consumption of anxiolytic drugs in the USA can testify (Bartolini, Bilancini and Pugno 2013). All these negative outcomes may induce people to call for policies, or even medicines, capable of "curing" them. To put it in general terms, the losers want to be protected.

As we will discuss in Chapter 4, the demand for protection has robust theoretical bases, rooted in behavioral and happiness economics, whereas the traditional arguments in favor of unregulated growth, which we will discuss in Chapter 2, turn out to be greatly weakened on the same bases.

Notes

1 See, e.g., Autor and Katz (1999), Goldin and Katz (2009), Acemoglu and Autor (2011).
2 "'Skill-Biased Technical Change' (SBTC thereafter) is a shift in the production technology that favors skilled, (e.g., more educated, more able, more experienced) labor by increasing its relative productivity and, therefore, its relative demand. Ceteris paribus, SBTC induces a rise in the skill premium – the ratio of skilled to unskilled wages" (Violante 2008, p. 2).
3 The conclusion that, in recent decades, technological progress increased the polarization of wage income, mainly affecting unskilled workers, was widespread albeit rather controversial. On this point, see Card and DiNardo (2002), Autor, Levy and Murnane (2003, 2006, 2008), Violante (2008), Dustmann, Ludsteck and Schönberg (2009), Acemoglu and Autor (2011), Autor and Dorn (2013), Freeman (2015) and Acemoglu and Restrepo (2016).

4 See, e.g. Autor, Levy and Murnane (2003), Acemoglu and Autor (2011).
5 On task-biased (and routine-replacing) technical change, see also Vivarelli (2014), Acemoglu and Restrepo (2017, 2019) and Gregory, Salomons and Zierahn (2019).
6 See, e.g., Katz and Murphy (1992), Autor, Katz and Krueger (1998), Autor, Levy and Murnane (2003), Wright and Dwyer (2003), Autor, Katz and Kearney (2006), Spitz-Oener (2006), Goos and Manning (2007), Autor and Handel (2013), Autor and Dorn (2013), Goos, Manning and Salomons (2014), Fernández-Macías and Hurley (2016), Sebastian (2018).
7 According to Campa (2017, p. 14), "Artificial Intelligence develops exponentially and not only promises to further reduce the workforce in manufacturing, but it will begin to erode the work of specialists in the service sector. In the near future, unemployment could concern economic actors who have attended higher education institutions and invested much time and money to acquire their professional skills, such as journalists, physicians, teachers, lawyers, consultants, managers, etc."
8 More in general, on the impact of lockdowns on global value chains see Ivanov (2020).
9 In the long run, the unemployment rate does not seem to be affected by the stringency of job protection legislation (OECD 1999, p. 50). Initially the OECD was much more inclined to consider employment protection legislation an obstacle to full employment (see OECD 1994); later that position changed: "the evidence of the role played by employment protection legislation on aggregate employment and unemployment rates remains mixed" (OECD 2004, p. 81).
10 The criticism of the positive role for employment of labor market liberalization is for example shared, albeit with different emphasis, by Bertola and Rogerson (1997), Garibaldi (1998), Agell (1999), Fitoussi et al. (2000), Blanchard and Landier (2001), Freeman (2005), Boeri and Garibaldi (2007), D'Orlando and Ferrante (2009), D'Orlando, Ferrante and Ruiu (2011).
11 For a thorough discussion of the impact of Employment Protection Legislation on the labor market and employment, see again D'Orlando and Ferrante (2009), and Chapter 4 in this book.
12 Quite similar conclusions can be reached within the endogenous money approach (Lavoie 1984; Palley 2001; Wray 2007) and by using some insights from this approach to address with the US financial crisis, as for example Stiglitz and Fitoussi (2009) try to do.
13 Modigliani's Life-Cycle Hypothesis is slightly different from Friedman's Permanente Income Hypothesis, but the underlying idea is quite similar, and also the mathematical formulation of the model is almost identical, so one can refer to the Modigliani–Friedman approach. See on this point D'Orlando and Sanfilippo (2010, pp. 1039–1040).
14 Rodrik (2016) argues that the speeding up of the process of economic transformation also resulted in a premature process of deindustrialization of low- and middle-income countries.
15 "We document a number of novel results. First, during our sample period individuals earn markedly different average returns on their financial assets (a standard deviation of 14%) and on their net worth (a standard deviation of 8%). Second, heterogeneity in returns does not arise merely from differences in the allocation of wealth between safe and risky assets: returns are heterogeneous even within asset classes. Third, returns are positively correlated with wealth: moving from the 10th to the 90th percentile of the financial wealth distribution increases the return by 3 percentage points – and by 17 percentage points when the same exercise is performed for the return to net worth. Fourth, wealth returns exhibit substantial persistence over time. We argue that while this persistence partly reflects stable differences in risk exposure and assets scale, it also reflects persistent heterogeneity in sophistication and financial information, as well as entrepreneurial talent" (Fagereng et al. 2020).
16 As we will argue later on (see section 4.4.3), tax havens and fiscal dumping played a relevant role in this context by reducing the capability to finance public expenditure.

17 "An important feature of our technology is that the skills produced at one stage augment the skills attained at later stages. This effect is termed self-productivity. It embodies the idea that skills acquired in one period persist into future periods. It also embodies the idea that skills are self-reinforcing and cross-fertilizing" (Cunha and Heckman 2007, p. 35).

18 The World Economic Forum's Global Social Mobility Index provides a assessment of 82 global economies according to their performance on five key dimensions of social mobility distributed over 10 pillars: 1. Health; 2. Education (access, quality and equity, lifelong learning); 3. Technology; 4. Work (opportunities, wages, conditions); 5. Protection and Institutions (social protection and inclusive institutions).

19 A study of the UK shows that, over the last 50 years or so, the chances of upward social mobility went down and the chances of downward social mobility went up and, as a result, the two probabilities converged for men to the same value of 35.8% (Bukodi et al. 2015).

20 Assuming utilitarian accounting where all individuals weigh the same.

21 "We find that relative income mobility is a significant predictor of life satisfaction and mental health. We also find that its effects are consistent with the loss aversion hypothesis – going down matters more. This is reflected in the fact that the coefficients attached to downward mobility are always larger than those for upward mobility" (Dolan and Lordan 2013, p. 16). For instance, according to Dolan and Lordan's estimates, the negative impact on life satisfaction of downward social mobility is 1.98 times the positive impact of upward social mobility.

22 In a recent contribution Milanovic (2020) "loses" the elephant: discussing the impact of the financial crisis on inequality, he reaches the conclusion that "[u]nlike in the case of the 'elephant chart' that very vividly caught the evolution of global distribution between 1988 and 2008, and where both the plutocratic top of the distribution and the 'new Asian middle class' grew at approximately the same rates, in the period 2008–2013, the top of the global income distribution grew cumulatively only by about 10% in real terms vs. more than 50% for the middle of the global income distribution. Even when we adjust highest national incomes for the likely underestimation, the growth of the top of the global pyramid increases to about 12–13% which is still far below the growth of the middle. This was one of the major effects of the global financial crisis: it arrested the exceptionally fast income growth of the richest people in the world. But it did not perceptibly affect convergence of mean country incomes, nor did it improve the relative position of Western middle classes whose income growth continued to be sluggish and to lag behind the world median" (Milanovic 2020, p. 37)

2 Traditional (optimistic) theories
Growth without regret

Underlying the deregulation policies implemented in the last few decades, and therefore also underlying the globalization process, rests the idea that by so doing the net benefits of innovation through creative destruction can be maximized. This argument is supported with mainstream theoretical models showing that the whole community would benefit from refraining from regulating the economy, i.e., not imposing constraints that limit the markets' allocative efficiency. These models are built within a standard maximizing framework founded on the hypothesis that subjects are fully rational and informed (or have rational expectations), whereas the psychological costs of (the absence of) intervention policies are barely considered.

This framework also implies an overestimation of the importance of long-period strategies aiming to boost economic growth, disregarding the role of short-period demand management and stabilization policies. Trying to summarize and simplify a complex problem, one might say that the post-war (Keynesian) approach derived from a short-period demand-side theory, whereas post-1980 (mainstream) theoretical support for globalization has been developed on the basis of a long-period supply-side theory. These two different theories almost inevitably reach very different conclusions. In particular, according to the latter, the economy inevitably gravitates around its long period trend, and demand management policies can only modify the size of the fluctuations around the trend. It is, therefore, no surprise that, according to the more recent approach, long-period growth, i.e., the attempt to raise the trend, should be the main goal of policy design. To obtain long-period growth the suggested strategies are supply-side policies based on market deregulation, tax cuts for firms and the wealthy, removal of barriers to free trade and capital movements across borders, liberalization of labor markets, etc. On the whole, these policies were thought to be capable of boosting the globalization process and the diffusion of technological progress, which was considered the main driver of economic growth. Thus, they have actually found implementation and characterize the strongest phase of the globalization process (which started around the 1980s).

These policies are often imputed with some serious drawbacks. In particular, (i) the choice not to implement stabilization policies could cause wellbeing losses for many subjects; (ii) tax cuts for corporations and the wealthy could increase

DOI: 10.4324/9781003018230-3

inequality and damage the poor; (iii) boosting technological progress and implementing liberalization policies could, in the age of robots and artificial intelligence, impact negatively on the labor market by generating technological unemployment; (iv) better results might be achieved if economic growth were accompanied by policies raising taxes to counteract inequality; and (v) if inequality increases, the risk is that the majority of the population may democratically vote for populist parties and movements whose aim is to reverse liberalization policies and ultimately stop globalization, making the entire mainstream growth strategy ineffective.

Well, according to the traditional approach all these drawbacks are actually nonexistent or at any rate highly improbable. In the following sections, we will discuss some of the reasons that mainstream economists adduce to support this conclusion.

In particular, in Section 2.1, we briefly describe the theoretical basis and historical evolution of the traditional (maximizing) approach, from the classical economists' theory to DSGE models.

In Section 2.2 we focus on deregulation and globalization, discussing the rationale for not increasing public intervention in the presence of cyclical instability, and illustrating the alleged positive consequences of the liberalization and deregulation processes for the poorest. In particular, these conclusions rest upon two main theoretical foundations. First, Lucas's argument (1987, 2003) holding that further macroeconomic policies seeking to stabilize the economic cycle are useless since the economic volatility caused by a reduction in public intervention has a small impact on consumers' wellbeing. Second, the trickle-down hypothesis (proposed by, among others, Dollar and Kraay 2002), which holds that liberalization policies and tax cuts aiming at boosting globalization might initially result in a higher income for the rich, but later something also trickles down to the poor, who therefore become less poor.

In Section 2.3 we describe the arguments of authors who maintain that technological progress resulting from liberalizations and tax cuts does not generate technological unemployment since a number of counteracting forces will prevent unemployment from increasing, in particular on the basis of the elasticity argument (defended by, among others, Blien and Ludewig 2017).

In Section 2.4 we deal with the idea that public intervention policies aiming at counteracting inequality reduce the rate of growth of an economy in so far as they levy taxes on productive investments (an idea proposed by, among others, Persson and Tabellini 1994; Lundberg and Squire 2003).

Finally, in Section 2.5 we describe the idea that the poorest do not oppose redistributive policies due to the "Prospect-of-Upward-Mobility" (POUM) hypothesis (proposed by Benabou and Ok 2001), so that there are theoretically robust explanations for the fact that populist policies have not so far stopped (and may possibly not stop in the future) liberalization strategies.

2.1 The traditional (maximizing) approach

The traditional maximizing approach has a long history that goes back to (at least) Adam Smith and his 1776 book *The Wealth of Nations*, but gained momentum mainly after the rise of the neoclassical theory, in the last decades of the nineteenth century, with the contributions by economists like William Stanley Jevons, Carl Menger, Leon Walras, and many others. Later this approach came up against major problems from the viewpoint of aggregate economic behaviors (i.e., macroeconomics) when faced with the Keynesian revolution (from 1936 to 1974). Nevertheless, it enjoyed a new lease of life, evolving and reaching full maturity, in the last decades of the twentieth century, after Nobel laureates Kenneth Arrow and Gerard Debreu gave it rigorous mathematical foundations in their Intertemporal General Equilibrium model. After Arrow and Debreu's contribution, the most radical aspects of the approach emerged fully in works by scholars like Nobel laureate Gary Becker, and later in the works by Nobel laureates Robert Lucas and Thomas Sargent. In particular, these latter economists, whom we met in Section 1.1.2 as the initiators of New Classical Macroeconomics, depicted the implications of the approach for macroeconomics and economic policy, contributing to building the *pars construens* of the theory (even though they also made an important contribution in questioning the logical basis of the Keynesian approach). Meanwhile, scholars like the Nobel laureate James Buchanan and Gordon Tullock, by developing the *Public Choice* approach, together with the similarly inspired theories of regulatory capture by Nobel laureate George Stigler, made a great contribution to the *pars destruens* of the mainstream approach, developing a radical critique of public intervention in the economy. The first versions of contemporary Dynamic Stochastic General Equilibrium (DSGE) models were also proposed in the 1980s. These latter models represent a step further in the Intertemporal General Equilibrium approach, achieved by adding the dynamic behavior of the system and random shocks. The most influential version of DSGE models was proposed by Nobel laureates Finn Kydland and Edward Prescott and is founded on the Real Business Cycle theory, according to which the shocks that hit the economy are always of a real nature (e.g., they can be caused by modifications in the quantity of productive factors or in their productivity). Another version, proposed by Julio Rotemberg and Michael Woodford, is on the other hand based on the hypothesis of monopolistic competition. Although some consider DSGE models a possible bridge between New Classical Macroeconomics and New Keynesian Economics, they are in fact very firmly rooted in the mainstream tradition, with maximizing subjects and perfect information (or rational expectations).

During the last century and a half, in spite of difficulties, crises and problems of various kinds, this rich and composite approach has dominated the theoretical scene, crowding out the great majority of alternative schools, and encompassing within its boundaries almost all the constructive criticisms made of it. Mainstream economic theory is still dominant today, and consequently is often referred to as the "orthodox" theory, or "traditional" theory, or simply as "neoclassical" theory.

Mainstream economics is based on the deductive method and is relatively simple in its logical structure. Starting from one single assumption and using logic (and mathematics), mainstream economists claim to be able to address any choice problem, whether within or outside the field of economics. The basic assumption of the theory is that subjects, in all circumstances, in every kind of choice they make, try to maximize their utility. According to the mainstream economists, subjects who want to maximize their utility are rational subjects, so that rational behavior and maximizing behavior are considered synonymous. In recent times, the theory evolved by building more sophisticated and robust foundations for rational behavior, the foregoing use of the (controversial and weak) concept of utility, even though ultimately utility maximization remains at the very basis of the approach. This point is worth stressing: there is no exception to it. The theory assumes that all subjects' behaviors are always driven by the endeavor to maximize utility. This maximization is constrained, in the sense that it is bounded by certain limits, but nonetheless, it always determines behaviors. Furthermore, it can easily be proven that if all individuals act selfishly in attempting to maximize their own utility, in a free, unregulated market the aggregate outcome is a social optimum. So, combining maximizing behaviors with free competitive markets, price signals, and price flexibility drive the economic system towards optimal equilibria implying full employment. Public intervention proves inappropriate, since the market itself is capable of reaching the optimal allocation of resources. Finally, wages are remuneration for the service of one of the three factors of production, namely labor, and are determined by the same criteria as the others, i.e., on the basis of marginal productivity. Since the marginal productivity of labor can be seen as the productive contribution of the workers, the workers receive a wage that corresponds to their productive contribution, and exploitation cannot exist: income distribution is inevitably fair.[1]

The assumption that subjects always try to maximize their utility, together with the full employment resulting from this behavior, has come in for a great deal of criticism. In particular, the criticism questions: (i) the hypothesis that people always seek to maximize their utility; (ii) the assumption that people possess the analytical skills necessary to solve the complex maximization problems of actual, real-world choices; and (iii) the possibility that people have the necessary amount of information to actually maximize. We will discuss these problems fully, together with the other weaknesses of the traditional approach, in Chapter 3.

Here let us simply recall that the debate was fierce in the 1990s and at the beginning of the twenty-first century, but mainstream economists have proved capable of successfully coping with all the criticisms that were leveled against the theory, in some cases by partially modifying its theoretical structure. In particular, the original assumption of maximizing subjects was modified to allow for the particular circumstances that could divert subjects from rational behavior, also considering the cases in which strategic behavior modifies behaviors, and the assumption of perfect information was modified by allowing subjects to possess (rational) expectations. Nowadays, most models are built to obtain probabilistic rather than deterministic results. However, all these modifications have left unchanged or have even reinforced the role of the maximizing behavior assumption.

In any case, rational behavior guarantees its optimality results and is therefore capable of justifying full employment and the stability of full employment equilibria (i.e., the ability of the system to regain full employment when a shock occurs) only when coupled with the assumption of free competitive markets: price and wage flexibility that characterize free competition are in fact the key starting point for justifying the ability of the system to regularly restore full employment.

In the following sections, we will focus on the way the assumptions of rational behavior and competitive markets allow mainstream economists to come to overoptimistic findings on the business cycle, economic growth, and the universal welfare-enhancing power of deregulation, tax cuts, and globalization, the (im) possibility of technological unemployment, the negative impact on growth and wellbeing of policies aiming to counteract inequality, and the attitude of the poorest in favor of remaining poor. According to the mainstream approach, growth is the road for raising wellbeing for everyone, and market liberalization and tax cuts are key to accessing that road.

2.2 The theoretical foundations of globalization and deregulation

Globalization and deregulation are two quite different phenomena that share a common basis, namely the idea that only freely competitive markets guarantee that the economic system reaches an optimum, so that policies aiming at reducing public intervention in the economy inevitably enhance global wellbeing. According to mainstream economists, this idea is not an a priori ideological assumption, but rather the conclusion of theoretical reasoning. Similar conclusions are obtained in many different ways and within many different contexts. In this section, we focus on the idea that (i) more public intervention is unnecessary when aiming at counteracting downturns, because downturns are temporary and neutral, and that (ii) economic growth benefits everyone, even the poorest, so that a reduction of public intervention that boosts growth ultimately improves economic conditions for all, including the poorest. Point (i) refers mainly to deregulation and countercyclical policies, while point (ii) has often been used to emphasize the positive effects of globalization (but also of domestic supply-side policies).

2.2.1 "Downturns are temporary and neutral"

The first point we discuss here is the role of stabilization policies. In this context, the question is: are public stabilization policies necessary and, more in general, useful?

Debate on the role of these policies dates back at least to 1987, when Robert Lucas published his book, *Models of Business Cycles* (Lucas 1987), and can be considered as concluded, at least in the building of mainstream theoretical conclusions (i.e., independently of the criticisms the approach has come in for) in 2003, when Lucas himself published the article "Macroeconomic priorities" on the *American Economic Review* (Lucas 2003).

The starting point of Lucas's reasoning is that "the general stabilization of spending that characterizes the last 50 years" (Lucas 2003, p. 11) has succeeded, since the "central problem of depression prevention has been solved" (Lucas 2003, p. 1). However, he wonders whether more aggressive stabilization policies, aiming at counteracting macroeconomic volatility, would have been useful. To be crystal clear, Lucas's contribution is not about recessions, which he sees as having

been overcome, but about the usefulness of counteracting macroeconomic volatility (i.e., the business cycle, random shocks that divert current economic outcomes from their long-period trend, and generate losses in consumption paths).
The underlining assumption being that demand-side stabilization policies can only
modify the size of the fluctuations of the economy around a (given) long-period
growth trend but not the trend itself, which is determined by supply-side forces.

Lucas considers further stabilization policies useless (if not dangerous) seeing that
"[t]he potential gains from improved stabilization policies are on the order of hun-
dredths of a percent of consumption, perhaps two orders of magnitude smaller than
the potential benefits of available 'supply-side' fiscal reforms" (Lucas 2003, p. 11).
Hence, supply-side policies, such as liberalizations and tax cuts, would be preferable.

Lucas's reasoning runs as follows. It is true that the business cycle affects people, generating losses in wellbeing. In particular, according to Lucas, people suffer two different kinds of losses: first, during economic downturns, people suffer
an objective loss caused by the reduction of their consumption below the long
period trend; second, people suffer a subjective loss caused by the impact that the
uncertainty about the (unpredictable) variability of their consumption during the
business cycle has on risk-averse subjects. However, again according to Lucas, in
a world of random shocks, the objective loss of wellbeing caused by downturns
can easily be offset by corresponding objective wellbeing gains caused by the
subsequent phase of expansion, when recovery drives the economy above the
long-period trend. But what about the loss in subjective wellbeing?

Lucas's main point is that the subjective loss is very small, so small that the
burden of the costs of further stabilization policies certainly exceeds their benefits. To arrive at this result, he calculates the utility loss caused by the business
cycle by comparing subjects' utility in the presence of random shocks and in the
presence of economic policies that eliminate these shocks.[2]

More in detail, Lucas considers the following intertemporal utility function,
in which utility depends upon a sequence through a time of actual consumption
expenditure, C_t, with t indicating the year:

$$U = f(C_t, C_{t+1}, \ldots)$$

with

$$C_t = (1 + \varepsilon) C^*_t$$

In these relations, C^*_t is the trend in consumption and ε is a random deviation
of actual consumption from the trend. On average, aggregate consumption corresponds to the trend but can be above or below it in a specific year. As pointed
out earlier, recessions affecting the trend are not considered.

The wellbeing loss suffered due to macroeconomic volatility can be measured
by the difference between the utility of a path of consumption closely corresponding to the consumption trend, $U = f(C^*_t, C^*_{t+1}, \ldots)$, and the utility of a path
of actual consumption deviating from the trend, $U = f(C_t, C_{t+1}, \ldots)$. Lucas
defines this loss as the amount of consumption that should be added to actual

consumption to obtain the same utility that a consumer would obtain in a world in which consumption did not deviate from the trend (Lucas 2003, p. 1).

Formally, we obtain this result by singling out the value of the cost of volatility μ that fulfills the following condition:

$$U((1 + \mu) C_t, (1 + \mu) C_{t+1}, \ldots) = U(C^*_t, C^*_{t+1}, \ldots)$$

According to Lucas, μ will increase with increasing consumption volatility and with increasing individual aversion to volatility. Hence, μ depends upon both the *objective* loss of consumption during the business cycle and individuals' *subjective* aversion to risk. Since (i) until 2007 consumption had not been particularly volatile, and (ii) Lucas assumes a relatively small risk aversion parameter, standing at one, he concludes that individuals would accept to pay less than 0.1% of their lifetime consumption to avoid volatility. It follows that policies aiming at avoiding further deviation of consumption from the trend are almost useless.

Lucas's contribution has come in for a certain amount of criticism, but most of these criticisms propose (small) theoretical modifications to the logic of the argument that do not greatly deviate from Lucas's quantitative results, thus leaving unchanged (or even strengthening) his main conclusions on the uselessness of policy intervention. This is, in particular, the case of the authors who argue that Lucas underestimates the cost of the business cycle due to his misanalysis of the relevance of risk aversion (see, e.g., Epstein and Zin 1991; Obstfeld 1994; Pemberton 1996; Dolmas 1998; Tallarini 2000). The only significant exceptions to these criticisms are the contributions that focus on the fact that Lucas excludes from his analysis not only a world in which macroeconomic instability is significant due to the absence of stabilization policies, but also the cases of great recessions, in which the problem is not simply random deviations from the trend (see, e.g., Salyer 2007). Exceptions, too, are the contributions (see, e.g., Krusell and Smith 1998; Mukoyama and Sahin 2006; Krebs 2007; Krusell et al. 2009) that criticize Lucas arguing that his use of the representative agent hypothesis prevents us from correctly estimating the (huge) impact of the business cycle on subgroups of subjects.

We agree with the latter two arguments, but the criticism of Lucas's approach that we propose in Chapter 3 is founded on different theoretical considerations and inevitably reaches different conclusions. In particular, we argue that Lucas greatly underestimates the wellbeing losses caused by downturns due to his incorrect calculation of "the non-pecuniary costs of unemployment (. . .), which typically increase during recessions" (De Neve et al. 2015, p. 19). We will base our conclusions on a number of robust theoretical and empirical findings from recent contributions in economics and psychology such as the concepts and models of *loss aversion, status quo bias,* and *hedonic adaptation.* Our findings will imply not simply that Lucas's contributions are numerically wrong, but also that his conclusions on the uselessness of stabilization policies should be reversed.

It is certainly true that Lucas discusses only the usefulness of more thoroughgoing stabilization policies than those actually implemented in the last few decades, concluding that they are unnecessary, and he does not suggest attenuating the intensity of these policies. And it is also true that his analysis does not apply to great recessions, such as the 2007 or COVID-19 crises. Nonetheless, his contribution has often been considered one of the many foundations for the mainstream common idea that public intervention policies are, in general, unnecessary in (almost) all circumstances, and as such it has to be discussed and criticized.

2.2.2 *"Growth is good for the poor"*

According to mainstream economic theory, not only should further stabilization policies be avoided, consistently with Lucas's ideas, but supply-side policies should be implemented, so as to boost economic growth, i.e. to modify the trend around which actual economic magnitudes fluctuate. Yet supply-side policies, as well as the resulting economic growth, have often been blamed for increasing inequality, so one might wonder whether everyone, including the poorest, can benefit from them. Therefore, before discussing the policies that can (as mainstream economists think) be implemented to boost growth, we should try to understand the effects of these policies on general wellbeing.

The trickle-down theory tries to answer the latter question. This theory, even in the absence of the support of any formal model, has often inspired policymakers and a number of policies implemented in both the developed and less developed countries at least starting from the 1980s, and stood at the center of theoretical interest in many debates on the benefits of globalization (see, e.g., Rodrik 2000; Dollar and Kraay 2002; Santarelli and Figini 2002; Bhanumurthy and Mitra 2004; Neutel and Heshmati 2006; Owyong 2010).

According to this approach, it is true that in boosting growth liberalizations, free-trade policies and tax cuts initially increase inequality, since the rich become richer.[3] But later on, after a certain increase in national income, inequality will diminish, because the increase of wealth trickles down from the rich to the poor.

The logic of the argument runs as follows. The policymaker implements supply-side policies, and in particular tax cuts for corporations and high-income earners, as well as deregulation policies for firms and banks; in the broader context of globalization and international trade the policies will focus in particular on liberalization of the movement of goods and capital across borders. However, both for countries implementing such policies mainly to boost internally driven growth, and for the (in particular, emerging and less developed) countries that aim to boost externally driven growth, the first result is a rise of income (and wealth) for the rich and thus an increase in inequality. But soon the banks will start lending more, the corporations will borrow more and make more investments, high-income earners will spend more, talented people will be stimulated to innovate due to the high returns on innovations, multinational firms will direct foreign direct investment to the country, exporting companies will invest as well, etc. Capital accumulation will raise productive capacity and will boost economic growth. The increase in investment, in exports, in consumption, and more in general in aggregate demand, will generate new and better jobs, more labor demand, and more employment, all circumstances that also benefit the low-income earners, i.e., the poorer. Furthermore, Growth will increase tax revenues and public expenditure on education, health, poverty reduction, etc., which also benefit the poorer. And "as more capital is accumulated in the economy, more funds will be available to the poor for investment purposes. This in turn enables them to grow richer" (Aghion and Bolton 1997, p. 151). So, ultimately, the economy will grow, and a share of this growth will trickle down from the rich to the poor.

As pointed out earlier, and apart from a contribution by Aghion and Bolton (1997), which touches upon rather particular cases, no robust economic theoretical model capable of describing in detail the logic of the approach exists, since the vast majority of contributions on the theme are by social and political scientists. The empirical confirmation is weak, too. However, in spite of this poor scientific interest and confirmation, many policies based on the trickle-down approach have been implemented, with mixed results.

2.3 The labor market

According to mainstream economists, technological progress is one of the main drivers of economic growth; it is boosted by free-market forces, and therefore favored by tax cuts, deregulation, and globalization. However, technological progress has often been blamed for crowding out employment: can this criticism also apply to contemporary technological progress, with robots and artificial intelligence entering into the production process? In Chapter 1, we maintained that in general economists are skeptical about the possibility that substitution of machines for workers can generate mass long-period unemployment, both in the past and nowadays. Mainstream economists, in particular, consider market forces strong enough to prevent technological unemployment. The skepticism of economists about the possibility of technological (full) unemployment is based on both theoretical and empirical considerations. Or it may be based on a thorough knowledge of the history of economic thought and the conviction that "this time cannot be different." In what follows we discuss, and criticize, the soundness of this idea.

2.3.1 *"If product demand increases enough there is no unemployment effect of technological progress"*

The theme of technological unemployment has long been at the center of interest of economic theory, at least from the years of the first industrial revolution. It was then that fear spread that the introduction of machines into the productive process might reduce human employment, generating technological unemployment. The idea was known as *substitution theory*, and was earnestly proposed by economists like Marx and, after initial hesitance, Ricardo.[4] However, many other economists defended a contrasting theory, known as *compensation theory*, according to which it was certainly possible that the introduction of machines increasing labor productivity in the productive processes might cause temporary unemployment, since the same amount of production could be obtained by hiring a smaller quantity of human labor. But the presence of human beings in the productive processes was in any case necessary, since machines could not substitute humans in all the tasks, and so could not alone accomplish the entire production process. Therefore, full unemployment was out of the question. But what about long-term mass unemployment?

According to the advocates of compensation theory, even if short-term unemployment was certainly possible, a number of forces, known as compensation forces, would soon come into action and restore the system to full employment. Among these forces we find automatic and deliberate intervention mechanisms, such as wage flexibility (which allows wages to fall in the presence of unemployment, thereby increasing firms' labor demand); reduction in production costs and prices (which cause an increase in the demand for goods, and in production and employment); increasing employment in the sector that produces the machines; product innovation, which creates new sectors of activity (and new employment in these sectors); the transition of employed humans from the primary (secondary) to the secondary (service) sector when jobs are destroyed in the primary (secondary) sector; increase in public expenditure, which increases aggregate demand, production and so employment, etc.[5] Although opinions on the topic vary, we believe we are not far from the truth in maintaining that the majority of economists considered these compensation forces effective in countering technological unemployment.

The theoretical conclusions on the impossibility of technological unemployment in the past have always been borne out by the empirical data and studies,[6] according to which although short waves of unemployment caused by technological progress were possible, long period technological unemployment was a phenomenon that had never come about in the past. On the contrary, the empirical data showed that in times of rapid technological progress, such as the New Economy Boom of the 1990s, unemployment tended to fall rather than increase.

In Section 1.1, we saw that there are some significant differences between the fourth and the preceding industrial revolutions from both the theoretical and empirical viewpoint. This is so since the entry of robots and artificial intelligence into the productive process today is crucially different from the entry of machines in the past. During the first industrial revolutions capital, i.e., machines, cooperated with labor in the productive process and raised labor productivity, so that the only problem was that a smaller number of workers were necessary to accomplish a given amount of production, meaning that unemployment could only rise if demand and production failed to rise sufficiently. However, robots do not cooperate with humans in the productive process but substitute human workers at a lower cost/productivity ratio, so that not only can a given production be accomplished with (almost) no human contribution, but increasing production does not necessarily require more labor: it might only require more robots, implying that unemployment may rise independently of demand considerations. Furthermore, any wage reduction that might allow the system to return to full employment could be hampered by the subsistence lower bound of the wage: indeed, the level of wages necessary for workers to be competitive with the cost/productivity ratio of robots may well fall below the subsistence level. In other words, traditional compensation forces are theoretically ineffective or at least need to be completely reconstructed and reconsidered. And yet economists seem to understate the risk of a situation in which, if new production is realized using robots alone, without the need to hire humans, human employment will not vary even if demand and production rise (see, e.g., Miller and Atkinson 2013).

All these do not imply that there are no compensation forces in the years of the fourth industrial revolution. Simply, it implies that these forces, if they exist, are crucially different from the compensation forces at work in the preceding industrial revolutions: it is possible that these forces may have to rely more on public intervention mechanisms and less on automatic mechanisms. In any case, the "old" theoretical conclusions on the effectiveness of the "old" compensation forces in restoring the economic system to full employment during the "old" industrial revolutions are useless when studying the effectiveness of the "new" compensation forces at work during the "new" (fourth) industrial revolution. As a result, new analyses need to be conducted. And there is absolutely no certainty that these analyses will reach the same conclusions as the old ones.

Actually, mainstream economists dedicate little effort to debating the theoretical challenges deriving from the fourth industrial revolution: most of them simply consider the results reached in the previous debate on the subject as valid also in the new framework, disregarding the great difference between a world in which machines cooperate with humans in the productive process (increasing labor productivity) and a world in which robots do not cooperate with humans but compete with them in taking on jobs. Furthermore, of the few economists that set out to evaluate the impact of robots on employment, in practice, the vast majority focus their (mainly empirical) studies on the increase in inequality caused by the third industrial revolution rather than the (potential) increase in unemployment deriving from the fourth.

The aforementioned considerations also imply that very few mainstream theoretical contributions address the fourth industrial revolution and its impact on technological unemployment.

Of the (few) mainstream models that might be used to tackle the subject, we find the models that study the similar problem of the impact of technological progress on the economy. These models are firmly rooted in the neoclassical general equilibrium tradition, with market-clearing equilibria and overlapping generations (see, e.g., Sachs and Kotlikoff 2012; Sachs, Benzell and LaGarda 2015; Berg, Buffie and Zanna 2018). Furthermore, in these models the idea that the wage has a subsistence lower bound is absent, all markets clear, and hence the problem is not unemployment but the level of wages or the labor share on income.

The problem with these models is that disregarding the existence of a subsistence lower bound for the wage undermines the possibility of using these models to address the impact of the fourth industrial revolution on unemployment, since wages do actually have a subsistence lower bound below which they cannot go. And, if robots are far more productive than humans, and their cost is not much higher than that of human workers, the wage reduction necessary to regain full employment may well drive wages below subsistence level – a level too low for human workers to accept employment. And the fact that almost all mainstream theories on the labor market have always disregarded the role played by the wage subsistence lower bound in the (wage) underbidding dynamics is by no means a good reason to disregard its role in the discussion of technological unemployment.

As in the case of the capital critique, the mainstream approach disregards the problems it is incapable of solving and carries on regardless.

Other mainstream models that can be used to address the subject of technological unemployment are the ones that focus on rebalancing mechanisms based on the flexibility of prices in the commodity markets. These models are all based on the traditional idea, first discussed by Neisser (1942), that the impact of technical progress on employment depends upon demand elasticity, so that "if product demand increases enough there is no unemployment effect of technological progress" (Blien and Ludewig 2017, p. 9).

Blien and Ludewig (2017), like other scholars proposing similar approaches (see, e.g., Combes, Magnac and Robin 2004), refer to a world in which technological progress may raise labor productivity and so, given produced quantities, induce firms to cut employment. By so doing firms reduce their production costs. The choice of this framework means that also these scholars tackle the consequences of the fourth industrial revolution with the tools that should be used to discuss the third, completely disregarding the great novelty represented by the possibility that robots endowed with artificial intelligence may not cooperate with workers but substitute them in the productive process. Within such a (disputable) framework, they argue that technological progress impacts firms' behavior in two ways: on the one hand, firms reduce employment, while on the other, thanks to lower costs, firms reduce prices, raising the demand for their production, and so production and employment. Thus, two counteracting effects caused by technological progress are at work, the displacement effect that increases unemployment, and the compensation effect that increases employment. The final impact on employment will depend upon which of the two forces is stronger. And the second force, i.e., the compensation effect, "is stronger the more price elastic demand is" (Blien and Ludewig 2017, pp. 8–9). So, according to Blien and Ludewig (2017, pp. 8–9): "If demand is elastic the compensation effect dominates, if it is inelastic the displacement effect prevails." Therefore, there is no technological determinism, and "[i]f product demand increases enough there is no unemployment effect of technological progress."

According to this latter approach, unemployment will therefore be higher in industries producing goods with a low demand elasticity, and lower in industries producing goods with a high demand elasticity. And no problem of technological unemployment would arise for the economic system as a whole.

This approach has two main drawbacks. The first is that it is an "old" approach, as pointed out earlier: it might apply to a world in which machines cooperate with human beings in the productive process, raising labor productivity, not to a world in which robots substitute human beings, since if production can be carried out using robots alone no employment increase will result from production increase. Second, according to other authors (see, e.g., Berg, Buffie and Zanna 2018; Bessen 2018), demand elasticity is diminishing over time, so that even if the use of robots reduces the prices of produced goods, the demand for these goods, and hence production and labor demand, does not rise, or shows only small increases. In any case, given a certain demand elasticity (and all the more so if the elasticity is low), the higher the substitutability ratio among robots and human workers, the lower is the strength of the compensating forces. If demand elasticity is particularly small, and in any case, if the substitutability ratio amounts to one, i.e., if production can be realized by robots alone, the compensation effect is ruled out and the traditional "elasticity argument" does not hold.

Different considerations, bearing nonetheless similar results, concern empirical studies. We have already emphasized the fact that the fourth industrial revolution has only just started, and its consequences for unemployment will be evident only in a couple of decades, so that empirical analysis is necessarily inconclusive, since at best it refers to the third and not the fourth industrial revolution. We cannot use empirical investigations with data from the past to discuss a different phenomenon that is happening/will happen in the future. At best such an analysis can confirm what happened in the last decades of the twentieth century (i.e., machines replacing unskilled/routine workers and increasing inequality), and cannot depict what will happen in the coming years. Nor can we assume that the future will be the same as the past. So, the absence of past empirical proof for a phenomenon that will happen in the future cannot be taken as proof that the phenomenon will not happen in the future.

More in general, and from a slightly different point of view, the question is: can the absence of empirical proof for the long-term consequences of a phenomenon that is beginning these days be considered adequate justification for denying the relevance and usefulness of developing theoretical analysis on the long-term results of that phenomenon? It is our conviction that the answer can only be in the negative. Theoretical analysis of relevant phenomena that are actually in their preliminary phases and might, or might not, come about in the future are perfectly legitimate and can – indeed must – be developed. Otherwise, we would not be in the particular situation that we have got into, a situation that sees everyone in the world, from social scientists to computer analysts (see, e.g., Brynjolfsson and McAfee 2011, 2014; Ford 2015; West 2015) discussing the problem of technological unemployment and its remedies, e.g., taxing the use of robots and implementing a universal basic income, while the economists discuss neither the problem nor the pros and cons of its possible solutions. We believe that economists should not limit their analyses to interpretations of past events which have a consolidated empirical impact. After all, economic theory possesses all the tools necessary to develop this type of theoretical analysis even if the empirical proof or disproof emerges only in the future.

2.4 Inequality and populism

As discussed in Chapter 1, the progressive rise and spread of populist parties and movements in many countries have often been seen as a side effect of the increasing inequality that, according to many scholars (see again Milanovic 2012), has hit these countries over the last few decades, and so as a side effect of liberalization policies and globalization.

Traditional theory deals with inequality, in a rather peculiar way, by maintaining that: (i) inequality can be a positive characteristic of an economic system and (ii) counteracting inequality could compromise economic growth.

2.4.1 Inequality boosts growth

According to mainstream economists, inequality does not necessarily generate negative consequences for economic performance, since it can increase aggregate demand and boost economic growth by generating incentives to work hard and invest (see, e.g. Mirrlees 1971; Lazear and Rosen 1981). This result is fully consistent with Kuznets's (1955, 1963) empirical studies, according to which economic inequality increases with initial economic growth (although it falls later on). However, inequality can in some respects be considered at the same time a consequence of and a prerequisite for economic growth. When the economy evolves from agriculture to industry, in the first phases of economic development, workers inevitably move from the primary to the secondary sector, and from the countryside to the city. The workers who move see their incomes increasing compared to the rest of the population, thereby intensifying inequality. Urbanization and higher income allow this wealthy class to provide a better education to their children and so increase their future incomes, further aggravating inequality but also boosting economic growth thanks to the greater accumulation of human capital. The role of inequality in boosting economic growth is also consistent with the idea of some scholars (see, e.g., Persson and Tabellini 1991) who hold that if subjects' propensity to save depends upon their income, and if the richer have a higher propensity to save, when the distributive share of the wealthy rises, the aggregate saving supply rises too, bringing the interest rate down and boosting investments, capital accumulation and economic growth. According to Persson and Tabellini (1991, p. 31), "at very low levels of development, redistributing income towards the rich may increase aggregate savings and hence lead to more rapid growth, if the rich have a higher marginal propensity to save than the poor." Furthermore, increasing inequality implies that some can become richer than others, and if people think that they can become richer they will invest more in human and physical capital, they will put more effort into their work, etc., thus also boosting economic growth.

However, the latter positive consequence of inequality will come about only in the presence of social mobility, i.e., if everyone has a chance to become richer. On the other hand, if people think that inequality depends upon their economic conditions at birth, so that the rich will remain rich and the poor remain poor, nobody will put more effort into their work and/or invest, and inequality consequently becomes a formidable obstacle to economic growth.

In the absence of social mobility, or in the presence of low social mobility, inequality is seen as a dangerous feature of economic systems, also because it could lead to social conflicts, political instability and uncertainty, hampering investments and economic growth (see, e.g., Alesina and Perotti 1994, 1996; Keefer and Knack 2000); or because it prevents the poor from accessing opportunities to borrow and invest, again hampering aggregate demand (even in the short term, see, e.g. Galor and Zeira 1993) and economic growth (see, e.g., Banerjee and Newman 1993; Lloyd-Ellis and Bernhardt 2000).

However, the most interesting implication of the traditional approach to inequality is the idea, largely shared by mainstream economists, that inequality is a negative feature of economic systems because, ultimately, it ends up forcing the policymaker to implement populist redistributive tax policies that hamper capital accumulation and economic growth. Therefore, it is not inequality that hampers economic growth, but the (populist) policies aiming to counteract it.

2.4.2 *"Counteracting inequality reduces growth"*

Although theoretical positions differ considerably among the different mainstream economists, their common idea is that inequality hampers economic growth in so far as it forces policymakers to implement redistributive policies. These policies most often consist of raising taxes for the wealthy, corporations, and banks, i.e. ultimately, directly and indirectly, taxing investment revenues. Taxing investment revenues reduces the incentive to invest, with the result of lessening capital accumulation and economic growth. Market regulation policies, such as adopting employment protection measures, imposing minimum wages, or stricter regulations on lending, have similar effects.

This idea is fully consistent with the "trickle down" hypothesis we discussed in Section 2.2.2. According to the "trickle down" argument, reducing taxes for the wealthy, firms, and banks, and implementing market liberalization policies, encourage firms to make investments and people to consume, raising aggregate demand and capital accumulation (in the form of physical, human, and knowledge capital). The opposite policy of raising taxes and implementing market regulation policies will obtain the opposite effect, reducing aggregate demand and capital accumulation. Therefore, the latter approach is simply the former proposed in different terms, adding the role of inequality as an incentive to raise taxes and market regulation.

The problem is that policymakers have difficulty in resisting the forces demanding redistribution: according to Acemoglu and Robinson (2002, p. 184), "capitalist industrialization tends to increase inequality, but this inequality contains the seeds of its own destruction, because it induces a change in the political regime toward a more redistributive system." "[T]hese political changes are induced by the rising social tension and political instability that arises from the increased inequality" (Acemoglu and Robinson 2002, p. 199). Therefore growth increases inequality, inequality boosts the demand for policies to counteract it, while policies to counteract inequality can easily turn into populist policies that reduce the incentives to capital and knowledge accumulation. Thus, not only does inequality contain the seeds of its own destruction, but also entails growth risks suffering the same fate.

The discouraging effect of populist policies affects all types of investment, but consistently with the endogenous growth theories, mainstream economists focus mainly on the damage that these policies can entail for "the accumulation of knowledge usable in production" (Persson and Tabellini 1991, p. 1). People devote resources to knowledge accumulation because they are confident that they can appropriate the fruits of this accumulation. But this possibility is linked to the level of taxation (and other regulatory policies) a country implements. With high levels of taxation the incentive for knowledge accumulation disappears, with the result that "[i]n a society where distributional conflict is more important, political decisions are likely to result in policies that allow less private appropriation and therefore less accumulation and less growth" (Persson and Tabellini 1991, p. 1).

The main theoretical result of this approach is that "income inequality is harmful for growth, because it leads to policies that do not protect property rights and do not allow full private appropriation of returns from investments" (Persson and Tabellini 1991, p. 30). Therefore, as we saw at the end of the previous section, according to mainstream economic theory it is not inequality that hampers economic growth: rather, economic growth is hampered by the policies aiming to counteract inequality.

2.4.3 The POUM hypothesis

One question, however, remains to be answered: in a democratic system the poor vote, so in the case of rising inequality how can policymakers evade implementing redistributive policies? Why should the poor not call for these populist policies?

The empirical and anecdotal evidence seems to confirm that in the developed countries the relatively poor majority of the population does not demand massive redistributive policies, i.e., does not call for policies to expropriate the rich few. Today there are signs that things are changing, but in any case, no full expropriation policy seems to be in sight.

It is not hard to see how, if the majority of (relatively) poor people who retain their political power call for massive redistribution, taxing the rich, corporations and in general investment revenues, liberalization policies designed to boost growth contain the seeds of their own failure: liberalizations boost economic growth; economic growth reduces poverty (if the trickle-down hypothesis holds true) but makes the rich far richer, increasing inequality; inequality may prompt the voters to call for massive populist redistributive policies; redistributive policies reverse the initial liberalization approach and discourage investments, reducing capital accumulation and putting a stop to economic growth. If this were the case, liberalization policies to boost growth would be ineffective, or even harmful.

Well, according to most scholars, and if a certain degree of social mobility is in one way or another ensured, a number of different mechanisms act in such a way that the aforementioned pessimistic scenario does not come true, since even the poor voters will not call for massive redistributive policies. This result is not a consequence of insufficient information, fallacious reasoning, overoptimistic expectations, or other psychological impediments, since if this were the case it would not be consistent with the very foundations of the mainstream approach. On the contrary, Benabou and Ok (2001) demonstrate that not voting for redistribution is fully consistent with maximizing behavior in a world where subjects have rational expectations. In Chapter 1, we described Benabou and Ok's POUM hypothesis and its empirical weaknesses. Here we will briefly consider whether their approach can represent one of the foundations capable of guaranteeing theoretical soundness for the mainstream approach.

According to Benabou and Ok (2001, p. 447):

> even people with income below average . . . will not support high tax rates because of the prospect of upward mobility: they take into account the fact that they, or their children, may move up in the income distribution and therefore be hurt by such policies.

They show that this "Prospect of Upward Mobility" (POUM) hypothesis also applies in a world where subjects are fully rational and so show maximizing behavior and rational expectations, given a number of assumptions, the most important of which being that "tomorrow's expected income is an increasing and concave function of today's income," i.e., "as current income rises, the odds for future income improve, but at a decreasing rate" (Benabou and Ok 2001, p. 449).

The conclusions reached by Benabou and Ok are in contrast with those arrived at by other authors (e.g., Alesina and Rodrik 1994; Persson and Tabellini 1994), since the latter maintained that the median voter would choose "high tax rates or other forms of expropriation," thus discouraging capital accumulation and economic growth (Benabou and Ok 2001, p. 452). In Benabou and Ok's approach, on the contrary, not calling for expropriation can be a fully rational attitude of the median voter.

Taking into account also Benabou and Ok's contribution, the whole mainstream approach proves consistent: liberalizations and tax cuts boost economic growth, economic growth benefits everybody, and even if inequality rises nobody demands the end of liberalization policies, which are thus self-sustained.

Our contemporary realities show us that even if inequality is rising in many developed countries massive redistributive policies have not been implemented, to some extent confirming the conclusions reached by Benabou and Ok. But much as is the case with technological unemployment, even if actual modifications in policies have not yet come about, populist movements, as well as parties proposing populist policies, are spreading in the world, gaining electoral consensus day after day. We still have no way of knowing whether this electoral consensus will actually translate into policies to counteract liberalization and globalization, but the tendency appears to be such.

Notes

1 For a thorough description of the characteristics of mainstream economic theory, see D'Orlando (2020a, p. 13).
2 "I ask what the effect on welfare would be if all consumption variability could be eliminated" (Lucas 2003, p. 3).
3 The increase in inequality is fully consistent with the dynamics depicted by the Kuznets curve. According to the empirical study proposed by Simon Kuznets (1955, 1963), income inequality increases with economic growth, reaches a maximum and thereafter falls. However, the direct link between inequality and economic growth in the first phase of economic development is challenged by some scholars. For example, as pointed out in Section 1.3.2, according to Aghion, Caroli and Garcìa-Peñalosa (1999), the cause of

increasing inequality is not economic growth but rather technological progress, which raises at the same time both growth and inequality due to skill-biased technical change.

4 For a description of the ideas of the classical economists on technological unemployment and substitution theory see, e.g., Feldman (2013), Vivarelli (2007), Campa (2017).

5 For a comprehensive list and summary of all the compensation mechanisms indicated by compensation theory, see D'Orlando (2020a, pp. 4–5).

6 A fairly complete description of these studies can be found in Vivarelli (2014), Gregory, Salomons and Zierahn (2019) and Calvino and Virgillito (2018).

3 The true costs of economic change

In Chapter 2, we discussed the theoretical bases of the idea that (i) economic growth is maximized under a free market regime, (ii) economic growth brings about benefits for all, (iii) stabilization and redistributive policies reduce growth, and (iv) technological unemployment is not a real issue.

In this chapter, we offer some arguments suggesting that the mainstream economists' overoptimistic ideas about the consequences of economic change disregard the true cost of this phenomenon and its allocation within society. In particular, we maintain that, even leaving aside its traditional, well-known and extensively debated weaknesses, mainstream economic theory suffers from a couple of other problems – given scant attention in the theoretical debate – which stand in the way of a thorough understanding of creative destruction, jeopardizing the soundness of its conclusions on the benefits of unregulated technological progress.

The first problem is a consequence of the high speed of the process of technological change caused by the third and fourth industrial revolutions. Indeed, the general wellbeing is negatively affected by the implications of the race between technology and education – with anticipated human capital obsolescence and increasing skill and educational mismatch – and by product cannibalization, with negative consequences for consumer satisfaction. Actually, in the absence of appropriate regulatory settings, the balance between the social costs and benefits of innovation has deteriorated in recent times due to the combined effect of a faster pace of creative destruction coupled with a low novelty content of innovations. On these grounds, we argue that the social reward of economic change should be reassessed through appropriate social metrics taking into account the considerable negative spillovers of creative destruction (Komlos 2014; Witt 1996). In this context, assessment of the consequences of economic change for consumers' and workers' wellbeing should factor in the main insights offered by behavioral economics.

The second problem, closely related to the first, is the inadequate way the traditional approach measures the wellbeing impact of market dynamics for subjects, and in particular for workers. The point here is that the traditional approach disregards all the psychological costs related to technological change, whereas once these elements enter the scene the true cost of creative destruction measured in terms of the general wellbeing rises sharply, and in particular it rises for the less

DOI: 10.4324/9781003018230-4

endowed (in skills and education). The rise of this cost radically changes the findings traditionally arrived at on the positive effects of uncontrolled technological change, with a consequent radical change of the conclusions on the usefulness of stabilization policies. Since the labor market is the most affected by innovation dynamics and deregulation, we focus on the consequences of creative destruction for workers' wellbeing, again making extensive use of some of the main instruments proposed by behavioral economics.

The chapter discusses these issues, emphasizing the inadequacy of mainstream economics to correctly assess the true costs of economic change and creative destruction.

In particular, in Section 3.1 we offer a concise lineup of the arguments that have traditionally been used to criticize a mainstream economic theory, distinguishing between the arguments directly related to its main assumptions (i.e., the idea that subjects always attempt to maximize their objective functions) and those related to its accessory assumptions (e.g., price and wage flexibility, competitive markets, representative agents).

In Section 3.2, we describe the technological paradigm shift brought about by the third and the fourth industrial revolutions, which calls for a critical assessment of the welfare costs and benefits of creative destruction, focusing in particular on the consequences of new phenomena of fast technological progress, product cannibalization strategies, and high product differentiation.

Section 3.3 deals with the impact of life changes on individuals from a socio-psychological perspective. The focus is on two aspects: (1) the difficulty individuals have in managing the "risk," uncertainty, fluidity, and "liquidity" typical of the current transformations; (2) the psychological and cognitive limitations that "inhibit" individuals, preventing them from making the most of change, even when it offers them a greater range of choices and possibilities.

In Section 3.4, we apply some insights from behavioral economics to support our analysis of the true costs of creative destruction for workers. Here we are referring to the implications for the experienced utility of loss aversion, the endowment effect, and hedonic adaptation.

In Section 3.5, we show why, and how, shocks more severely affect those who have less and who suffer greater wellbeing losses from creative destruction, magnifying the negative impact of technological progress on aggregate wellbeing. Building on this conclusion we maintain that the traditional economic analysis, which disregards the true wellbeing losses determined by technological progress, cannot represent a sound basis for dismissing public intervention policies.

3.1 The main weaknesses of the traditional (maximizing) approach

In the previous chapter, we maintained that critics of the traditional theory mainly focus on three weaknesses in this approach: (i) the hypothesis that people always want to maximize their utility; (ii) the assumption that they have the analytical skills necessary to solve the complex maximization problems of actual, real-world choices; and (iii) the possibility that they have the necessary amount of information to actually maximize. All these points relate to the soundness of the crucial assumption of maximizing behavior, which is at the very basis of the theory. However, other accessory assumptions, often but not always present in mainstream theoretical models, weaken the approach. In particular, we may mention the realism of the assumption of price flexibility, the unrealistic importance attached to the idea of perfectly competitive markets, and the questionable role attributed in most macroeconomic models to the simplifying hypothesis of representative agents. In this short section, we focus on the three main traditional and extensively debated criticisms (i)–(iii), i.e., on the soundness of the idea that subjects want and are able to maximize their objective functions. In the following sections, we will raise rather different criticisms, all but absent in the theoretical literature, which use behavioral economics to demonstrate how greatly the traditional approach undervalues the (negative) impact of contemporary technical change on aggregate wellbeing – with the consequence that mainstream economists' policy suggestions are inevitably baseless.

In contemporary economic debate two main schools of thought have discussed the aforementioned theoretical issues: Behavioral Economics (based on the works of scholars like Amos Tversky and Nobel laureates Herbert Simon, Daniel Kahneman, Robert Shiller, and Richard Thaler), which focuses mainly on points (i) and (ii), and New Keynesian Economics, which focuses mainly on point (iii). These two approaches have different basic assumptions and structures, but often overlap and arrive at similar results.

Behavioral Economics focuses on the study of the cases and circumstances in which subjects do not behave rationally, i.e., do not attempt to maximize their objective functions, but rather follow different choice behaviors, such as routines or rules of thumb, since they do not possess the analytical skills necessary to actually maximize or are subject to biases that prevent them from maximizing. The aim of scholars who share this approach is to propose a microeconomic foundation for human behavior alternative to the maximizing one, based on insights from cognitive psychology, whereas their opponents claim that they simply succeeded in indicating some very specific exceptions to rational behavior. Unlike the traditional approach, behavioral economics does not rely on a sole principle (maximization under constraints) to derive all the different behaviors of agents. Instead, this approach recognizes a multiplicity of determinants for human behavior, each offering the best fit in a specific circumstance (Rabin 2002). This flexibility brings the scholars closer to actual economic behavior than traditional theory, albeit at the cost of greater difficulty in developing a unitary theoretical framework. The approach is based on a great amount of seminal contributions which, according to some scholars, go back to Keynes's ideas (see, e.g., D'Orlando and Sanfilippo 2010). The most important of these seminal contributions were published between 1947 (see, e.g., Simon 1947) and 1979 (see, e.g., Kahneman and Tversky 1979), but the theory reached worldwide recognition only in the nineties.

The other approach, New Keynesian Economics, shows little uniformity in its contributions, ranging from the study of the labor market to study of the financial markets, and uses different models and assumptions, but its most important theoretical strand focuses on the availability of information in a world where subjects still want to maximize their objective functions.[1] Actually, New Keynesians do not reject, and indeed often explicitly accept, the assumption of maximizing behavior, but they deny that maximizing behavior is by itself capable of generating a social optimum (and hence full employment). As a result, public intervention is necessary. They obtain this result by removing one of the foundations of the definition of freely competitive markets, namely perfect information, and introducing a new cause of market failure, namely asymmetric information. As pointed out earlier, the New Keynesian approach shows scant consistency, being made up of different sectoral models designed to explain the functioning of single specific markets, and in particular the labor market and the credit market. Among the major contributions on the labor market, we find the implicit contract model (Azariadis 1975; Baily 1974), the insider–outsider model (Lindbeck and Snower 1984), the efficiency wage model in its two versions of moral hazard (Shapiro-Stiglitz 1984) and adverse selection (Weiss 1990) and the monopolistic syndicate model (Oswald 1986; Dunlop 1944). Of the main contributions that study the credit market, the credit rationing model proposed by Stiglitz and Weiss (Stiglitz and Weiss 1981) is particularly relevant. In all these models, we find wage, interest rate, and/or employment rigidity, and these rigidities prevent the system from reaching the full employment equilibrium and so call for public intervention. These models differ from the neoclassical synthesis ones insofar as they do not derive the rigidities from reality but on the contrary explain them on the basis of the maximizing behavior of subjects in a framework in which information is incomplete and/or asymmetrically distributed.

In what follows we will extensively use insights from behavioral economics to evaluate the psychological costs of creative destruction but will make no further reference to the criticisms that behavioral economists level against maximizing behavior, since our method, and our conclusions, are quite independent of the *pars destruens* of this theory.

3.2 Creative destruction revisited

There is no doubt that innovation and creative destruction (see Section 1.2) are basic ingredients of economic growth and essential conditions to improve productivity and general wellbeing. Creative destruction enhances productivity through Darwinian selection and by stimulating competition and innovation among incumbent firms. The issue we discuss here is whether the costs of economic change should be reassessed owing to the changing nature of the latter process, as described in the following.

The leading scholar of innovation, Joseph Schumpeter, was well aware of the costs imposed by creative destruction on the "losers" and stressed the need to support the orderly retreat of the latter to prevent their reaction against and opposition to dynamics considered beneficial for society as a whole. However, the economic and technological scenarios which Schumpeter confronted and which prevailed until the 1960s were very different from those which subsequently came to prevail. As a general case, Fordist production technologies and firms' internal organization did not need highly skilled workers, so workers could then be easily transferred from one firm/sector to another. The life cycle of technology, industries, and products was longer. Demand for skills was more predictable and stable. Most of the innovations introduced had a significant impact on the shift in the demand schedule because they contributed to satisfying basic needs and solving serious economic and social problems. Resource mobility across countries, and in particular the mobility of capital, was limited. Consequently, the rate of economic change through creative destruction was much slower, and anticipated physical and human capital obsolescence was not a real challenge for most workers or society. The race between technology and education was not an issue and the skill and educational mismatches were not the serious social and economic problems (Autor, Goldin and Katz 2020) they are today (World Bank 2019).

The sources of turbulence stemming from creative destruction should not be attributed solely to firms' entry in and exit from the market and the resulting occupational dynamics.[2] Market dynamics due to technological innovation include other changes in firms' strategies resulting from their need to adapt to rapidly changing environments. The increase in temporary employment is simply the main symptom of the latter strategy of adaptation. Outsourcing on a global scale, including externalization of R&D activity through open innovation, is another consequence of the pursuit of flexibility which, eventually, led to a redistribution of value-added and the risks of economic activity within value chains in favor of the global players.

In the previous chapter, we discussed in depth the negative impact of today's technological progress on unskilled workers (and/or on workers performing routine tasks). But if unskilled workers are the main losers and victims of the new institutional and technological regime, the remaining part of society, and specifically, consumers, are not necessarily the beneficiaries. Long ago Scherer (1979) provided a very effective description of market dynamics that may lead to a negative balance between the costs and benefits of product innovation for society – a story that can usefully be generalized to assess the main consequence of the very fast innovation processes and industry dynamics we are now experiencing. The main point he stressed, in relation to the analysis of the *Ready to eat cereal industry*, is that most of the innovative activity that took place in the industry brought about product *cannibalization* and did not appreciably improve consumer welfare. Oligopolistic competition in the industry relied on strategies of investment in new products with small innovative content but requiring a large outlay in advertising with the goal of signaling and amplifying the novel content of the new products. The resulting process was, essentially, one of *cannibalization* where the overall costs (innovation plus advertising costs) exceeded the consumer benefits measured through the shift of the demand curve.

The probability of competition through innovation generating such an inefficient outcome is not confined to oligopolistic competition and is related to three factors: (1) the actual contribution of innovations to the increase in consumers' welfare, i.e., their innovative content; (2) the cost of innovating, including the cost of signaling the innovative content and (3) the speed of introduction of innovations. The first factor affects the demand schedule (the extent of the shift) and the resulting increase in consumer welfare. The second factor affects the cost borne to develop the innovation and make it available to society. The latter includes not only the R&D costs borne by the innovator but also the investment made by unsuccessful competitors. Duplication costs are just one, although the main side of the story. Advertising and marketing expenditure by innovators and their competitors is another. Finally, the third component includes the cost of anticipated depletion of the physical and human capital of displaced firms and workers.

This point is particularly relevant: the workers might not be the only losers. The consumers' human capital can also be depleted due to fast economic change: with asymmetric information about the quality of goods there are heavier learning costs for consumers, in particular, in the case of goods and services requiring more specialized user skills; these costs include the search costs and the costs to learn how to enjoy the novelty content of new goods (Di Giacinto and Ferrante 2007). Due to rapid change, the latter is often not fully exploited, thus reducing the value of innovations to consumers: when they get to know the full potential of new products, yet newer versions enter the scene.

The mainstream economic theory fails to recognize this crucial aspect. At the heart of the theory lies the idea that expanding options is always a good thing, that learning costs for consumers are negligible and that choices are based on unbiased predictions of the hedonic experiences associated with them (Ferrante 2009):

> The economist's traditional picture of the economy resembles nothing so much as a Chinese restaurant with its long menu. Customers choose from what is on the menu and are assumed always to have chosen what most pleases them. That assumption is unrealistic, not only of an economy, but of Chinese restaurants. Most of us are unfamiliar with nine-tenths of the *entrées* listed; we seem invariably to order either the wrong dishes or the same old ones. Only on occasions when an expert does the ordering do we realize how badly we do on our own and what good things we miss.
>
> (Scitovsky 1992, pp. 149–150)

The main limit to rational choices stems from the fact that "people do not always know what they will like; they often make systematic errors in predicting their future experience of outcomes and as a result fail to maximize their experienced utility" (Kahneman and Thaler 2006, p. 3). Such systematic errors emerge even in very simple decision settings involving very short timespans (Kahneman and Snell 1990, 1992).

Unregulated and fast economic change entails not only direct costs for consumers, workers, and firms in declining sectors but also indirect costs for society as a whole which have been underestimated so far. Leaving aside the need to provide support for the "losers" (unemployment benefits, active labor market policies, and other welfare programs) a rapid process of change also brings about anticipated

skill obsolescence. The social returns of past investments in education and training are adversely affected and the cost of updating skills is borne mainly by society at large (due to the need to revise school curricula and provide continuous
training to the workers). The private costs are only a small part of the social cost
of economic change due also to the distortions entailed by the need to finance at
least part of education and training programs through general taxation.

It is evident that shorter product and technology life cycles, due to a more
intense process of creative destruction, inevitably compromise the social reward
of innovations by increasing their overall costs and reducing their benefits.

3.2.1 The social reward of innovation when cannibalization
is pervasive: a more formal treatment

Simply speaking, the social reward of innovation r_s is given by the net present
value of the increase in social welfare (increase in consumer's surplus CS plus pro-
ducer's surplus) over the total social cost of innovating. The latter includes private
and public costs of R&D, $R\&D_0$; the fixed (private) investment cost to implement
the new technology, K_0; the cost of retraining workers, TC_0; the costs for compensating the "losers," C_0; and the learning costs imposed on consumers, LC_0:

$$r_s = \frac{\sum_{t=1}^{T} \dfrac{\Delta CS_t + \Delta \pi_t}{(1+i)^t} - (SC_0)}{(SC_0)}$$

$$SC_0 = K_0 + R\&D_0 + TC_0 + C_0 + LC_0$$

where π is profit and T the average shelf life of the new innovative product.

For instance, suppose that the initial competitive market equilibrium is (P', Q')
in Figure 3.1. To simplify things, suppose that process innovation is a public good
provided by the government[3] to all firms so that all of them can charge a lower
post-innovation competitive price amounting to P'. In the new equilibrium, all
the firms remain in the market and workers keep their jobs. The increase in social
welfare is given by area $CBDE$. If process innovation is associated with product
innovation, shifting demand from DD to DD', the increase in social welfare is
given by area $CFMC'E$. In this simple case:

$$r_s = \frac{\sum_{t=1}^{T} \dfrac{\Delta CS_t}{(1+i)^t} - (K_0 + R\&D_0 + TC_0 + LC_0)}{(K_0 + R\&D_0 + TC_0 + LC_0)}$$

Of course, r_s will be increasing in T and ΔCS (change in consumer' surplus, i.e.,
the innovative content of technical change), and decreasing in the direct and indirect costs of innovation. With this simple setting, we can assess the consequences

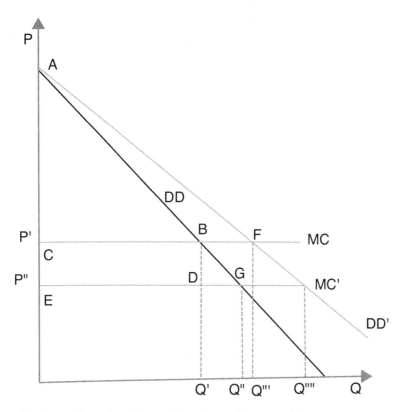

Figure 3.1 The welfare gains of innovation under perfect competition.

for the social reward of innovation of a more intensive process of creative destruction characterized by incremental innovations with little innovative content.

Innovations, whether due to an incumbent firm or a new entrant, are not a public good and tend to crowd out incumbent firms and their workers. Deadweight losses due to noncompetitive pricing by innovators are just a small part of the story. Some firms will see early obsolescence of their assets and workers' skills. At least temporarily, the unemployed workers will bear most of the cost and will eventually need to be retrained to find a new job. These costs are largely borne by the public sector, i.e., the taxpayers who, in addition, have to bear the burden of social insurance and other welfare programs. The sort of labor market flexibility required by this innovative environment will entail pecuniary and nonpecuniary costs for the workers that increase with an increase in the rate of change.

Intensive innovation activity based on product differentiation also brings about other consequences that may reduce the social returns to innovation.[4] The idea that expanding work and consumption opportunities *always* increases people's wellbeing is well established in economics, but it finds no support in psychology (Ferrante 2009; Schwartz et al. 2002; Schwartz 2000; Roese and Summerville

2005). The point is that, whereas an expanded set of choices is good for *decision utility*, it may not be good for *experienced utility*.[5] But why is this so? A wider range of opportunities extends people's freedom to choose, but expanding options also implies psychological decision costs:

> First, there is the problem of gaining information about the options to make a choice. Second, there is the problem that as options expand, people's standards for what is an acceptable outcome also rise. And third, there is the problem that as options expand, people may come to believe that any unacceptable results are their own fault, because with so many options, they should be able to find a satisfactory one. Similar problems arise as choice becomes available in domains in which previously there was no choice.
>
> (Schwartz et al. 2002, p. 1179)

Regret mirrors the latter costs that people bear over their life courses: "Opportunity breeds regret, and so regret lingers where opportunity existed" (Roese and Summerville 2005).

3.3 The impact of change on individuals: a sociopsychological perspective (by Albertina Oliverio)*

In the last few decades, Western society has seen unprecedented transformations and innovations in science, technology, economy, and society at large. The impact of change on individuals, in terms of costs and benefits, has long been studied from various perspectives in the social sciences. In sociology, in particular, many authors have reexamined the work of classical thinkers on the transition from more traditional societies – characterized by strong social cohesion, scant division of labor, and strong common values – to modern societies, characterized by a high degree of specialization and complementary functions in labor, a weakening of the collective consciousness and an increase in individualism. These aspects of social change were, in different ways, what thinkers like Emile Durkheim (1893) had in mind when distinguishing between the "mechanical solidarity" of the past and the "organic solidarity" of modernity; Ferdinand Tönnies (1887), contrasting the "community" of the past with modern "society"; and George Simmel (1900), highlighting the connection between the growing individualization of modern society and dependence on the monetary value of money.

Now, many decades since the founding fathers of sociology discussed these issues, one of the most studied issues is the capacity of individuals to adapt to the many profound changes that characterize contemporary society. Attention has often focused on the costs of this adaptation. In the present study, we will focus on two aspects in particular: the first is the difficulty individuals have in managing the risk, uncertainty, fluidity, and "liquidity" typical of current transformations; the second is the psychological and cognitive limitations that inhibit individuals, preventing them from making the most of change, even when it offers them a greater range of choices and possibilities.

Let us examine these questions more in detail. Human beings have always had to cope with the risk and uncertainty associated with change. However, in contemporary society, these appear "amplified" by the continuous changes occurring in work, lifestyle, social and family relations, free time, and so on. All this makes our existence "fluid": mutable, unstable, uncertain. In a word, "liquid." Liquidity is the characteristic of a new phase of modernity in which all the foundations, the certainties, the superior forms of authority typical of early modernity and of traditional societies have been undermined (Bauman 2000). A good part of these transformation processes is the direct result of scientific-technological innovations. Now, it is obvious that in one way these innovations offer advantages over the past, allowing us to reduce the risk and uncertainty in many areas of human existence and enhance the autonomy of individuals, allowing them better to control, manage and make decisions in various areas. Consider, for example, the way the relationship with the body has changed: the idea of a body subject solely to nature, typical of the past, has been replaced by the idea of human control, for the purpose of reducing risk and uncertainty, as well as the anxiety they generate. Thanks to progress in medicine, pharmacology, and genetics, individuals have greater control over the functioning of their bodies (prevention and cure of diseases, assisted maternity, etc.), and other innovations also offer control over the body's external appearance (cosmetics, aesthetic surgery, etc.). Another area that has seen enormous innovation is communication, where technology has radically changed individuals' relations with space and time. Spatial and temporal distances have been reduced or eliminated, offering the possibility to intervene directly on many problems. The capacity to manage one's life has been augmented, creating a sense that one can dominate time, appropriate it, control it, and manipulate it.

On the other hand, the continuous changes that have characterized our existence also have negative and occasionally paradoxical consequences, which should not be underestimated and have a significant impact on the capacity of individuals to adapt to transformations.

Without going so far as to subscribe to a catastrophic interpretation of scientific-technological change, it is obvious that progress and innovations have always entailed costs, giving rise to reservations in many thinkers. The great philosopher Günther Anders (1956) articulated these reservations in his reflections on "Promethean shame," the shame we feel when confronted with the "humiliating quality degree" of the objects we produce. Anders was writing in the middle of the Cold War, when people were in the grip of the fear of the "bomb," the new device with which humans, the new Prometheus, threatened to wipe out the entire human race. In more recent years, critics of the contemporary age like Anthony Giddens and Ulrich Beck have spoken of a "society of risk," arguing that many contemporary disasters would not have come about without the "progress" made possible by science, that many scientific innovations are what makes it difficult or impossible to manage and control risk and uncertainty, the very thing science had promised to do.

Here risk becomes a key concept for an understanding of transformation in advanced industrial society (Beck 1986): risk is increasingly a product of human action (i.e., nuclear energy, mad cow disease, asbestos, contaminated blood, genetically modified organisms, etc.); it creates the need for new scientific developments, which in turn generate new forms of risk. This circularity thus has unforeseen consequences, new social dangers, and problems, which engender anxiety and fear.

But aside from these more obvious causes, current feelings of anxiety, fear, and malaise are also fueled by another consequence of change: the increased range of choices and possibilities. On the one hand, this greater range of choices is, obviously, positive – it grants us greater control over our existence than in the past, when many choices were dictated by society (education, marriage, children, etc.). On the other hand, there are also negative consequences: the disappearance of traditional forms of belonging has created a growing individualization that forces us to be continuously making choices, and this pressure to choose can become an imposition, a tyranny, engendering psychological and cognitive difficulties.

Returning to innovation in communication, for example, while it is true that in a way it has "liberated" individuals from the constraints of time and space, and increased their chances of taking autonomous decisions, there are also a series of negative consequences. Individuals today are "dominated" by time and often have trouble establishing priorities, distinguishing the essential from the accessory, the important from the only apparently urgent. They are obsessed with urgency and end up choosing intensity over duration, immediate results over future ones, without worrying about the consequences. The logic of urgency and the new technologies thus create the illusion that we can abolish time and create the space to do more things than before. An illusion, as we said, because the result is, on the one hand, that time is "overloaded," as an increasing number of activities are crammed into it, and, on the other hand, these human activities lose their more profound significance, remaining associated with an ephemeral present at the expense of meaningful future prospects.

In this context, urgency becomes a form of "perversion of time" (Aubert 2003) resulting in a number of pathologies typical of our society. Among these are many of psychosomatic disorders including headaches, insomnia, back pains, herpes, eczema, psoriasis, heartburn, and other gastrointestinal pathologies, as well as depression of varying gravity. This is the burden of what has been termed the "insufficient man" (Ehrenberg 1995), the man who suffers because he does not feel himself up to the world and is unable to respond adequately to external pressure. Sometimes these pathologies lead to what has been called a "corrosion" of personality (Sennet 1998), through nervousness, aggressiveness, and rage, which have negative consequences on work performance. At other times, the problem concerns the relation with other individuals which become superficial and ephemeral: a "short-term society," in which everything is related to the present and social relations are confined to a brief and unstable horizon.

The use of cell phones and smartphones today is one of the most evident manifestations of this "cult of urgency." Smartphones make us more independent and at the same time closer to others. They are, of course, devices that liberate from the constraints of time, offering individuals a sort of permanent ubiquity that allows them to be in more places at once, to accelerate time, to choose when to communicate, to manage multiple situations simultaneously without having to be in a specific place. The immediacy of smartphones, however, also has "perverse effects" on modes of communication. The desire to be effective, direct, essential, leads to a rapid, immediate communication. We communicate much more than before and with more interlocutors, but conversations on average are more superficial (consider for example a typical WhatsApp chat).

Along with the development of an "economic" lifestyle, requiring ever-increasing flexibility, efficiency, and immediacy, the massive spread of these communication technologies and of instantaneous communication modes has had a noticeable impact on interpersonal relations, which have become increasingly "fluid": detached and uncommitted. While in the past stability was socially and culturally appreciated, today it is associated with rigidity, and flexibility has become decisive (Sennett 1998). Society has developed in which individuals "exist insofar as they are connected," making subjective existence dependent on the outside and relations with others. This may become a dependency, even a pathological dependency, on certain modes of communication (smartphones, chats, social networks), and tends to undermine more lasting and profound relations (Bauman 2003).

Scientific-technological change and innovations thus produce an increase in the choices available but, as we have seen, this can lead to a form of constriction that generates psychological and cognitive problems. It is commonly assumed that happiness and satisfaction are the results of being free and that being free means being able to choose among a vast range of alternatives. Yet, there is a threshold beyond which an increase in individual autonomy, in the possibility of choosing (goods, information, entertainment, innovations, etc.), can have a negative effect (Schwartz 2000, 2004). This is another paradoxical consequence of the level of change characterizing Western society: the high degree of expectations created by the abundance of choices available to the individual often ends up generating anxiety, dissatisfaction, fear, uncertainty, insecurity, and passivity. To reaffirm their identity and autonomy fully, contemporary individuals must be continuously making choices, but this often results in psychological malaise, and the inability to decide and to devise the cognitive mechanisms needed to address these new social demands (Iyengar 2011; Salecl 2010). A well-known study on the motivations behind choices has shown that subjects were less likely to purchase a given product when offered a higher number of variants to evaluate (24 flavors of jam), compared to others offered fewer options (6 flavors). The study also evidenced that the first group experienced less satisfaction and greater frustration. In particular, the group with the higher number of choices showed regret at having been unable to find the perfect flavor (Iyengar and Lepper 2000).

This fear of making the wrong choice can therefore "inhibit" choice. Thus, a greater range of choices does not necessarily mean satisfaction, since individuals become more afraid of making the wrong choice and yet regret not having made one. On the other hand, psychologists are well aware of the human tendency to look for "reassurances," in order to avoid facing uncertainty, risking disappointment, or having to acknowledge the existence of unpleasant facts or facts that clash with their beliefs. This common tendency can lead to what in cognitive psychology is called "confirmation bias." Beyond this lies a more general epistemological problem associated with what are known as ad hoc hypotheses. The epistemologist Karl Popper (1935) explained how, in science, one should avoid trying to save a pet theory at all costs by taking for granted hypotheses that supported it in order to avoid its falsification. In everyday life too, we often tend to make this mistake and try to confirm our hypotheses at all costs. To understand how confirmation bias works we can consider the following classic example.

A sample of students was presented with the following test (Wason and Johnson-Laird 1972).

The four cards represented in the picture each have a number on the side and a letter on the other. Someone tells you: "The cards with vowels on one side have an even number on the other. Which cards should we turn up to find out whether the person is lying?"

The most common reply was "E and 4," followed by "E." Only a few students answered correctly "E and 7." Most students were trying to prove the statement that had been made. In reality, they had been asked to "falsify" the "if x then y" statement (if the card has a vowel on one face, then it will have an even number on the other). But the only way to falsify such a statement is to find a case of "x and not y" (vowel and not even). The only cards that falsify the statement are those with both vowels and uneven numbers, the others (cards with consonants and even numbers, consonants with uneven numbers, vowels with even numbers) are irrelevant.

Confirmation bias is a cognitive mechanism commonly used to reduce the anxiety generated by the fear of making the wrong choice. It exists alongside two other psychological mechanisms used by contemporary individuals to cope with change: the reduction of cognitive dissonance and social confirmation.

Based on the "cognitive dissonance" mechanism (Festinger 1957), when an individual is faced with dissonant alternatives, i.e., with alternatives that are equally attractive (smoking is pleasurable, stopping is good for you) or equally undesirable (not marrying or marrying a person with different religious beliefs), he/she will try to "reduce" the dissonance either by changing his/her beliefs, or by reinterpreting the contradictory information without abandoning his/her beliefs. Everyone, based on their experiences, knowledge and opinions, has certain expectations of reality, and if faced with a fact that undermines them, might prefer to modify their perceived reality rather than their expectations.

"Social proof" (Cialdini 2006) is another psychological mechanism used to reduce the uneasiness caused by the difficulty of choosing: it entails "trying to discover what others consider right" and behaving accordingly. This can lead to conformist attitudes or purely imitative behavior, promoting "massifying" tendencies that paradoxically coexist with the drive towards individualization typical of our society.

This type of psychological mechanism and the resulting behaviors can be interpreted as efforts by today's individuals to adapt to change and innovations that are constantly occurring in society, and, as we have seen, heighten the need to find certainties, values, stability, serenity, and security, loss of which is all too often the price we pay for a change.

3.4 Labor market: the costs of flexibility[6]

In the previous chapters, we stressed that the ultimate impact of the transformations that have occurred in the last forty years or so is a more intense process of creative destruction that also brings about greater turbulence in the economy and, specifically, in the labor market. The continuous upgrading of technology, mainly due to the implementation of new solutions based on ICTs and, specifically, on AI, the development of new business models and the introduction of new goods and services have modified the entire chain value and displaced firms and workers within countries and at the global level.

This process has been facilitated by relaxation of employment protection legislation in almost all the OECD countries, in particular for temporary contracts (Figure 3.2). Not surprisingly, in the same period, the share of temporary contracts increased from 10% to around 15% of dependent employment (see Figure 1.3, Chapter 1).

In the previous chapters and sections, we discussed the impact of shocks and policies on the labor market: in particular, deregulation of the capital market, combined with lack or imperfect mobility of workers and together with the impact

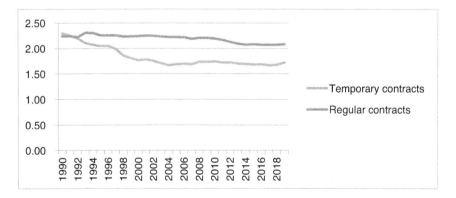

Figure 3.2 Index of strictness of EPL for temporary and regular contracts, 1990–2019

Source: OECD database

of the third and fourth industrial revolutions, have been responsible for a general tendency for working conditions to worsen, particularly for the lower-skilled workers, but also for workers in the middle of the skills distribution in OECD countries. The threat of global competition, like a phantom, became a mechanism leading to the reduction of the workers' bargaining powers on the global scale.

Perfect capital mobility also brings about faster processes of reallocation of production activity on a worldwide scale through direct foreign investments. On the whole, in addition to speculative capital movements, this more intense process of creative destruction brings about greater uncertainty in all the spheres of people's lives, and in particular in working conditions and the need to continuously adapt to a changing environment. Faster obsolescence of skills and the need to be retrained is just one side of the story. People must adapt to a changing world and may find a limit in their cognitive skills and ability to confront uncertainty, in particular in the case of individuals with poorer educational backgrounds. It is jobs and the labor market that are most affected by this rapid process of change and the average unemployment rates do not capture the true nature of these dynamics and the increasing precariousness and decreasing quality of job positions affecting, in particular, workers in the middle and lower brackets of the skills distribution. Generally speaking, a more dynamic labor market forces individuals to anticipate more frequent unemployment episodes. And these unemployment episodes bear heavy pecuniary and nonpecuniary costs.

3.4.1 Pecuniary and nonpecuniary costs of flexibility

The increasing precariousness of jobs implies, among other things, that individuals are forced to anticipate more frequent job changes in their working life and more frequent unemployment episodes. Unemployment episodes, and more in general precariousness and labor market dynamics, bear heavy costs. These costs can be usefully divided into pecuniary and non-pecuniary components. In particular, studies on happiness suggest that unemployment episodes entail both a pecuniary and a nonpecuniary cost:

> the lower subjective wellbeing of unemployed people can be explained neither by the lower income level nor the self-selection of intrinsically less happy people, unemployment has to be related to non-pecuniary costs. The drop in happiness may be attributed to a large extent to psychological and social factors.
>
> (Frey and Stutzer 2002, p. 420)

Pecuniary costs can be computed in monetary terms and are the income and/or consumption losses deriving from unemployment, the costs of searching for a new job, the costs of geographical mobility, the possibility of finding a new job with a lower wage, etc. Nonpecuniary costs, on the contrary, are not associated with a loss of income and/or consumption but include the psychological costs that subjects suffer due to changing status, habits, and lifestyles, potential social stigma, loss of esteem, and social networks, etc. These psychological costs must be measured in terms of wellbeing rather than consumption (and/or income).

The wellbeing losses caused by unemployment are particularly painful, since unemployment is one of the most negative outcomes in life (Clark and Oswald 1994; Frey and Stutzer 2002), and the same inevitably holds true for anticipation of more frequent unemployment episodes, i.e., greater precariousness. Subjects appear incapable of fully recovering from the loss of wellbeing determined by unemployment episodes, even if they receive full income replacement, and even if they find a new job. In their study on happiness, Di Tella, Haisken-De New and MacCulloch (2007) argue that people can adapt to income shocks completely but that their adaptation to life's events is incomplete.[7] And in a context of greater precariousness, not only unemployed people suffer from the wellbeing losses caused by unemployment, but also employed people perceive a greater risk for future episodes of unemployment and suffer wellbeing losses, in particular, if social safety nets are not available and the expected quality of reentry job is worse.

Behavioral economics greatly contributed to raising awareness of the nonpecuniary components of the costs of facing a turbulent labor market which the standard approach to decision-making generally ignores and that are related to some phenomena examined in economic psychology. Inclusion of these factors and analysis of their cultural determinants allow for a more robust assessment of the costs of flexibility and its connection with workers' skills and education (D'Orlando and Ferrante 2009; D'Orlando, Ferrante and Ruiu 2011). The basic intuition is that education, in addition to positively affecting actual employment opportunities, mitigates the adverse effects of personal traits, such as fatalism, on workers' perception of employment and income opportunities. On these grounds flexibility (or inflexibility) is a behavioral attitude of individuals that is affected primarily by culture and education, and not a normative characteristic of labor markets.[8]

Of the numerous principles discussed in behavioral economics, the most important for our analysis are those associated with changes of status and the costs of changes of status, i.e., the *status quo bias* (Samuelson and Zeckhauser 1988; Kahneman, Knetsch and Thaler 1991), the *endowment effect* (Knetsch and Sinden 1984; Knetsch 1989; Kahneman, Knetsch and Thaler 1990, 1991), *loss-aversion* (Tversky and Kahneman 1991; Kahneman, Knetsch and Thaler 1991), and *hedonic adaptation* (Clark and Oswald 1994; Frey and Stutzer 2002).

Many behavioral studies have focused on the *status quo* bias and the *endowment effect*. The two concepts are closely linked and also linked with the idea that people are more responsive to losses than to gains of equal proportions.

The *status quo* bias was originally described by Samuelson and Zeckhauser (1988), who found a strong preference of individuals for the *status quo* (or for what they believe is the *status quo*) "because the disadvantages of leaving it loom larger than advantages" (Kahneman, Knetsch and Thaler 1991, pp. 197–198). A somewhat similar behavioral principle, namely the *endowment effect*, has been verified empirically, mainly through repeated experiments (see e.g. Knetsch and Sinden 1984; Knetsch 1989; Kahneman, Knetsch and Thaler 1990). We can describe the *endowment effect* as "the fact that people often demand much more to give up an object than they would be willing to pay to acquire it" (Kahneman, Knetsch and Thaler 1991, p. 194). When an object becomes part of the subject's endowment (and here is the link with the *status quo* bias), the subject tends to overvalue it.

Both the *status quo* bias and the *endowment effect* can be explained with the concept (and theoretical framework) of *loss aversion*. *Loss aversion* has the advantage of being theoretically founded upon the *prospect theory* by Kahneman and Tversky (1979). According to Kahneman, Knetsch and Thaler (1991, p. 199):

> [a] central conclusion of the study of risky choice has been that such choices are best explained by assuming that the significant carriers of utility are not states of wealth or welfare, but changes relative to a neutral reference point. Another central result is that changes that make things worse (losses) loom larger than improvement or gains. The choice data imply an abrupt change of the slope of the value function at the origin.[9]

The *status quo* bias resulting from *loss aversion* represents the first step (albeit, as we point out in the following sections, not the only one) in construing why the traditional approach greatly undervalues the negative consequences of economic change in unregulated markets. According to this behavioral principle, adverse economic outcomes that hit a subject generate a huge negative impact that favorable economic outcomes of the same magnitude cannot fully offset. Therefore, for the particular case of the labor market, the psychological cost of frequent job losses, with the consequent loss of a given standard of living, in an unregulated market, maybe greater than evaluated in the mainstream approach, and greater than the cost of waiting longer for a new job in a regulated market. And the perception of the loss is presumably also affected by the fear that the reentry job will be worse. Furthermore, since both the ability to adapt to changing conditions and the quality of the re-entry job tend to be less for lower-skilled workers, the expected cost of unemployment due to *loss aversion* is, on the whole,[10] greater for a worker with less human capital.[11] The mainstream economic theory takes into account only monetary losses, and not psychological losses, and therefore disregards all these excesses of loss, greatly undervaluing the negative consequences of flexibility.

The idea that *loss aversion* is not a fixed innate characteristic of individuals finds empirical support in Johnson, Gachter, and Hermann (2006), who show that it is decreasing with education or, more generally, with (?) knowledge endowment; age also has a strong negative impact. Overall, the best interpretation of these empirical findings is that the *status quo* bias is related to the ability of subjects to adapt to changing external conditions.

Loss aversion can also explain why social mobility may be less important than is claimed in determining political aversion to redistribution (Benabou and Ok 2001). With *loss aversion*, the positive expectations of gains from upward social mobility may well be offset by the negative expectations attached to even very small probabilities of downward social mobility. Individuals holding these beliefs may thus rationally decide to bargain in the labor and political markets for stringent job protection.

Finally, *loss aversion/status quo* bias has also been cited by Fernandez and Rodrik (1991) to explain why "governments so often fail to adopt policies that economists consider to be efficiency enhancing" (Fernandez and Rodrik 1991, p. 1146). Contrary to rent-seeker models, which posit that the few gainers from the *status quo* are politically stronger than the many losers, Fernandez and Rodrik adopt the hypothesis that "there is a bias toward the *status quo* (and hence against efficiency-enhancing reforms) whenever (some of) the individual gainers and losers from reform cannot be identified beforehand" (Fernandez and Rodrik 1991, p. 1146). Even if the reform yields gains for the majority of subjects, ignorance of the crucial matter of who will gain and who will lose generates resistance: "when individuals do not know how they will fare under a reform, aggregate support for reform can be lower than what it would have been under complete information, even when individuals are risk-neutral and there is no aggregate uncertainty" (p. 147).

3.4.2 Hedonic adaptation to unemployment status?

The last and probably far more important behavioral principle that can be used to assess the impact of unemployment and precariousness on workers' wellbeing is hedonic adaptation. Set-point theories of subjective wellbeing and empirical and experimental evidence suggest that people react to positive and negative life events, but then return to initial levels of happiness and satisfaction over time (Clark et al. 2004). This phenomenon is known as *hedonic adaptation*. The evidence is that *hedonic adaptation* does work also in the case of unemployment but that the process is not complete. The same conclusion is reached by Clark et al. (2004, p. 8):

> We test this idea by examining reaction and adaptation to unemployment in a 15-year longitudinal study. In accordance with set-point theory, individuals first reacted strongly to unemployment and then shifted back toward their former (or 'baseline') levels of life satisfaction. However, on average, individuals did not completely return to their former levels of life satisfaction, even after they became re-employed. These findings suggest that even a short period of unemployment can cause an alteration in a person's long-term set-point.

The hedonic adaptation framework is also useful for evaluating the different roles (and weights) of pecuniary and non-pecuniary shocks, since Di Tella, Haisken-De New and MacCulloch (2007) and Easterlin (2004) find strong empirical support to the idea that people adapt more easily to pecuniary shocks than to the nonpecuniary effects of changing status. The authors suggest that adaptation to income shocks is complete but that adaptation to life events is incomplete.

On the whole, the evidence suggests that the fixed nonpecuniary cost of unemployment episodes may be more important in determining wellbeing than the variable pecuniary cost of relatively protracted joblessness:

> Although the baseline of life satisfaction was relatively stable for individuals from before to after unemployment, the experience of unemployment did on average alter people's baseline. At the aggregate level, people were less satisfied long after unemployment, suggesting that the event lowered the average set point of these respondents (. . .) Our findings suggest that an unemployment experience might scar people in some way that they are less satisfied with life on average even after re-employment and even controlling for income.
>
> (Clark et al. 2002, pp. 12–13)

As a consequence, the income that would be necessary to compensate people for the loss of wellbeing due to unemployment is very large and, according to many authors (see, e.g., Winkelmann and Winkelmann 1998; Di Tella, MacCulloch and Oswald 2001, 2003; Frey and Stutzer 2002), implies a replacement ratio much greater than one.

Figure 3.3 illustrates the time-path of the wellbeing of a typical worker in the presence of *loss aversion* and *hedonic adaptation*, at constant wage income. After the first episode of unemployment, subjective wellbeing falls dramatically; thereafter, wellbeing slowly increases through *hedonic adaptation* but never regains its original level, even if the subject gets a new job. Each subsequent unemployment episode reduces the set-point of the worker's wellbeing.[12] The process is cumulative – even if the irreversible loss is progressively smaller at each episode due to long-run *hedonic adaptation* – and the total extent of the irreversible loss

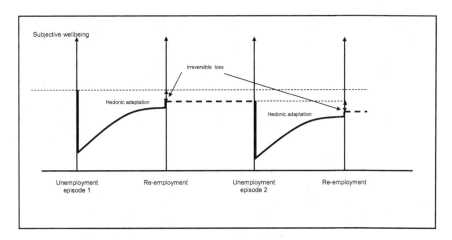

Figure 3.3 The time path of a worker's wellbeing with *loss aversion* and *hedonic adaptation* (with constant income when employed)

in wellbeing is a concave function of the number of unemployment episodes. As a result, the negative impact of many short unemployment episodes on wellbeing is greater than the impact on wellbeing of few long unemployment episodes. Mainstream economic theory, by taking into account only the monetary and not the psychological costs of unemployment, fails to capture this excess of loss caused by unemployment episodes. So that, again, it greatly undervalues the true costs of unemployment and precariousness.

3.4.3 The cultural determinants of loss aversion and hedonic adaptation

In the preceding section, we maintained that the process of hedonic adaptation in the case of unemployment episodes may be incomplete, preventing subjects from returning to the baseline level of wellbeing after a negative, job-loss shock and generating an irreversible wellbeing loss. And the negative psychological impact of employment shocks is particularly relevant for people with lower educational and skill endowments. This is so for at least three reasons. First, because the workers with lower educational attainment are more likely to be fired, so in an unregulated labor market they would suffer a greater number of unemployment episodes and hence a greater cumulate irreversible wellbeing loss caused by incomplete hedonic adaptation. Second, because people with lower education suffer a greater loss aversion (Johnson, Gachter and Hermann 2006; D'Orlando and Ferrante 2009) so that for them the process of hedonic adaptation after an unemployment episode is "more" incomplete, i.e., the cumulative loss deriving from *the same number* of unemployment episodes is greater than for the more highly educated people. Furthermore, they (correctly) anticipate being subject to a higher unemployment risk for the future, and this perception, too, lowers their wellbeing. Thus, they suffer triple damage.

The higher level of loss aversion and the consequent incompleteness of the hedonic adaptation process for the lower educated (low-skilled) workers can be linked to underlying differences in culturally based beliefs and, in particular, according to D'Orlando and Ferrante (2008, 2009), and D'Orlando, Ferrante and Ruiu (2011), to different levels of *fatalism* and *trust in others*. Fatalism and trust in others depend not only upon subjects' innate socio-economic backgrounds and cognitive skills, but also, and mainly, upon non-cognitive traits acquired through education. It is, therefore, the poorly educated individuals that are most affected by these culturally transmitted beliefs. For these subjects, loss aversion is particularly strong and so the cost of unemployment particularly heavy due to the powerful impact of the psychological component: fatalists see themselves as being unable to cope with drastic negative changes in life. In other words, *fatalism* raises the nonpecuniary, psychological costs of unemployment – a utility loss that does not disappear even if the income loss is entirely offset by unemployment benefits.

The fact that loss aversion and hedonic adaptation have cultural and educational determinants also implies that the impact of unemployment and precariousness on wellbeing varies greatly between countries and even regions. In the latter case, when there are different cultures and different levels of fatalism within a single country, the policymaker has the problem of mediating between the different needs and cultures which inform the electoral body and the working force. Political mediation generally solves these heterogeneity problems with side payments, and this solution works until the differences become too great. In this case, the parties that reject political mediation and call for federalism as a means to reconcile the cultural heterogeneity with the institutional and political homogeneity of the country enjoy considerable popularity among the voters. The heterogeneity may also become so great that no mediation remains possible. In such a case cracks can open in the unity of the State, so that different regulations (and in particular different labor market regulations) apply to different areas of the country.

3.4.4 Economic change and the cost of geographical mobility: a neglected issue

In a frictionless world, workers move from obsolete shrinking sectors to innovative, expanding ones and bear no mobility costs. Real life is very different. There is no guarantee that new jobs will be available in the same location where the workers and their families live and have put down their roots. In a globalized world, workers should be ready to move far from their original location to new provinces, regions, and even countries. If there are two or more workers in the household, the consequences are even more serious.

The American model of rootless workers is not necessarily positive from the point of view of the workers' and their families' wellbeing. Moving around means that solid relationships cannot be formed with other people. The connections within families are weakened and individuals cannot count on the support of their families when needed, in particular whenever social protection nets are not available.

The support of the social network and families is important not only in bad times but also in normal times, providing important services to families that they cannot afford on the market, e.g., nursing and babysitting, or which are not provided by the public sector. More generally, social connections are a major ingredient of subjective wellbeing. Bartolini, Bilancini, and Pugno (2013) argue that the decline in social connections experienced in the USA after the 1980s is responsible for the observed fall in subjective wellbeing, i.e., in peoples' happiness.[13]

The long-term consequences, for society as a whole, of individuals with weak roots can be serious. The motivations to act in a cooperative way – an essential ingredient of well-functioning communities – are closely bound up with identification with the community. If this link is weakened, competition between individuals may prevail in society, thus leading to widespread social conflicts. The traditional approach to economic change is also unable to capture these impacts on wellbeing.

3.5 The disproportionate impact of creative destruction on those who have less

Our main conclusion up to this point is that the negative psychological impact of employment shocks has a particular effect on the lower educated and less skilled people. This conclusion follows from the circumstance that for these subjects loss aversion is particularly strong, since *fatalism* raises the non-pecuniary, psychological costs of unemployment.

All these points apply in general. Does anything change if we consider more specifically the kind of shocks we discussed in this book, and in particular the business cycle, recessions, and the impact of technological progress on the labor market in its twofold manifestation, i.e., skill/task biased technological change (third industrial revolution) and technological unemployment (fourth industrial revolution)?

Let us start with the business cycle. During business cycles economic magnitudes gravitate around their long-period trend: sometimes above the trend, sometimes below. However, and unlike recessions, on average the actual magnitudes roughly coincide with the trend. But even if over time negative and positive outcomes cancel one another out *in the aggregate*, this is not the case with single subjects. During downturns some subjects experience no modification in their economic position, others find their economic position improved (at least in relative terms), while yet others find their economic positions worsened (in absolute and/or relative terms). Since there is no certainty that those who lose during downturns are the ones that gain during the successive recovery, at the end of an entire business cycle some will have gained and some will have lost. But losers and winners are not randomly distributed – random shocks do not randomly affect different categories of subjects. On the contrary, during downturns, those less endowed in terms of skills, education, and wealth face a higher probability of being negatively affected than those who have more and a lower probability of gaining during recovery. Furthermore, those who have less often failed to regain the same income (and consumption level) that they had before the downturn, so that even with a nil average variation of income over time, the less endowed suffer irreversible losses in monetary terms. In other words, and simplifying a little, shocks always affect (mainly) the same (poor) people, and recoveries often affect (mainly) the same (rich) people. According to Mukoyama and Sahin (2006, pp. 19–20), "[u]nskilled agents face more cyclical unemployment risk and they have less opportunity to self-insure. As a result, the cost of business cycles is much larger for a typical unskilled agent compared to a typical skilled agent."[14]

One might argue that, in any case, the losses suffered by the losers are offset by the gains obtained by the winners, so that aggregate variation for the whole community during a complete business cycle is nil. However, this may be true in monetary terms, but not in psychological terms. Indeed, the fact that downturns negatively affect the less endowed (in terms of skills and education) more, and that it is they who suffer more from *loss aversion*, generates a double loss for the economic system as a whole: because the losses outweigh the gains, the wellbeing gains of the winners do not offset the wellbeing losses of the losers, so that the aggregate wellbeing is reduced. Moreover, as the losses mainly hit the less endowed (again, in terms of skills and education), and it is the less endowed that suffer greater wellbeing losses for a given negative shock, aggregate wellbeing also diminishes for this reason. The resulting aggregate wellbeing variation for the economic system as a whole may therefore be considerable and negative.

Furthermore, in such a context the losers suffer not only the wellbeing losses directly caused by falling wages but also the wellbeing losses caused by positional effects. By positional effects we mean the impact that differences in income (or consumption, or wealth) among subjects exert on wellbeing, the idea being that increasing (negative) differences reduce a subject's wellbeing even if her/his absolute income (or consumption, or wealth) does not change, and even if it rises in monetary as well as real terms. These phenomena have in particular been studied in theoretical models of preferences for status, conspicuous consumption, envy, and escalation (see, e.g., Veblen 1970; Chaudhuri 1985; Hammond 1989; Mui 1995; Kolm 1995; Grolleau, Mzoughi and Sutan 2006; D'Orlando and Ricciotti 2021). The prevailing idea in these studies is that positional effects generate wellbeing losses and negative externalities (see, e.g., Frank 2005; for different conclusions see D'Orlando 2021).

The business cycle, and its impact on the general wellbeing, was a highly topical issue during the last decades of the past century, and in particular in the period between 1980 and 2007, when the dominant idea was that economic policy had succeeded in stabilizing the economy. Not by chance, this period was called "the Great Moderation," and economists wondering whether to recommend more active intervention policies often answered in the negative (as we have seen, for example, referring to Lucas's ideas). Things radically changed at the turn of the century. The first warning was the bursting of the technological (dot.com) bubble. From then on the world economy has been hit by three consecutive crises: the (second) Great Recession, the Eurozone crisis, and the COVID-19 crisis. All three of these crises can hardly be seen as the contraction phase of an economic cycle, and for many countries, they have caused not only a temporary contraction of gross domestic product but also an irreversible reduction of the growth rate. So the question is, can the considerations we proposed here referring to the business cycle be extended to the case of Great Recessions?

The answer is affirmative, since there is no significant change in the logic of the argument, and our conclusions are in fact strengthened in the case of greater economic shocks, in particular, if these shocks happen repeatedly in a short time. In these cases not only do frequent unemployment episodes hit the subjects with many irreversible and cumulative wellbeing losses caused by the incompleteness of the hedonic adaptation (habituation) process, but the frequency of the shocks also greatly aggravates their insecurity with regard to the future, so that the fatalists more affected by recessions may think that there is no hope for them. Fatalism increases and wellbeing losses multiply.

However, both the business cycle and great recessions are somewhat transitory shocks (even if, in the case of great recessions, they are capable of permanently affecting the rate of economic growth). Technological progress is a different kind of shock, capable of generating a permanent and increasing impact on economies and, in particular, on unemployment, via the two connected but different phenomena of skill (or task) biased technological change and robotization.

Unlike the case of business cycles and recessions, in the case of skill-biased (or task-biased) technical change subjects face not only temporary unemployment and/or temporary wage reduction, but also a *permanent* wage reduction in both absolute and relative terms. In this case, positional effects matter far more, since skill (or task) biased technical change *permanently* lowers labor demand and wages for some categories of workers, while leaving unchanged or even raising labor demand and wages for other categories of workers with consequent permanently increased inequality and hence envy towards those who retain or ameliorate their wage level. These are some of the consequences of the third industrial revolution, and they are permanent, thus marking a crucial difference with the consequences of the (temporary) shocks represented by (temporary) downturns caused by the business cycle and recessions: low-skilled workers, or workers undertaking routine tasks, know that they have no (or very few) chances of improving their relative position in the future.

The negative effects of technological progress prove even greater, and by far, on turning to the consequences of the fourth industrial revolution, when technological progress will not simply reduce labor demand and wages, leaving unemployment almost unchanged, but will permanently increase unemployment, aggravating the wellbeing losses of (fired) workers. In such a context subjects know that they have no real chances of moving up to higher grade consumption behaviors, earning a higher wage, or even any wage. Therefore, other negative effects on their wellbeing will come on top of those described as a consequence of unemployment due to the business cycle, recessions, etc. Their wellbeing will also fall because of more limited aspirations, and/or due to subjects' awareness that their aspirations are impossible to realize (on this point see, e.g., D'Orlando 2021, section 3).

Notes

* Dipartimento di Scienze Giuridiche e Sociali, Università G. D'Annunzio Chieti-Pescara.
1 The other principal strand of New Keynesian approach is based on the existence of market imperfections that prevent the system from reaching full employment equilibria.
2 Thus standard measures of labor market turnover may not capture these intensified dynamics (Akcigit and Sina 2019; Aghion et al. 2016).
3 So that we can leave welfare losses out of the picture due to noncompetitive equilibria and R&D duplication cost.
4 R&D duplication costs borne by unsuccessful competitors should also be included in the picture.
5 *Decision utility* is inferred from choices and used to explain choices, whereas *experienced utility* refers to the hedonic experience associated with an outcome (Kahneman and Thaler 2006, p. 2). Experienced utility and life satisfaction are used interchangeably.
6 This section is largely based on D'Orlando and Ferrante (2009, 2018), and D'Orlando, Ferrante and Ruiu (2011).
7 On this point, see also Easterlin (2004).
8 Whereas culture cannot be modelled by politicians and takes a long time to change, education can be managed through appropriate policy measures (see Chapter 4).
9 Another brilliant description of Kahneman's and Tversky's *prospect theory* is the following: "Their theory exploits a 'value' function, rather than a utility function. This value function is centered at the *status quo* (the 'reference point'); it is defined over deviations from the *status quo*; it is kinked at the *status quo*, being concave for gains and

convex for losses; and it is steeper for losses than for gains. As a result, the value function exhibits risk-averting behaviour in choices involving sure gains and risk-seeking behaviour in choices involving sure losses" (Hartman, Doane and Woo 1991, p. 142).

10 The pecuniary loss due to involuntary unemployment should be greater for more skilled workers earning higher wages.

11 Guiso, Jappelli and Pistaferri (1999) estimate that 72% of Italian college graduates face a zero probability of unemployment episodes whereas the same percentage for poorly educated workers drops to 57%.

12 "Individuals first reacted strongly to unemployment and then shifted back toward their former (or 'baseline') levels of life satisfaction. However, on average, individuals did not completely return to their former levels of life satisfaction, even after they became re-employed. The findings suggests that even a short period of unemployment can cause an alteration in a person's long-term set-point" (Clark et al. 2004, p. 8)

13 "[. . .] the decrease in happiness is mainly predicted by the decline in social connections and by the growth in reference income. More precisely, the sum of the negative changes in happiness predicted by the reduction in social connections and the increase in reference income more than offsets the positive change predicted by the growth of household income" (Bartolini, Bilancini and Pugno, 2013, p. 123).

14 According to the data reported by Mukoyama and Sahin (2006, pp. 4–5), unskilled workers ("high school diploma or lower") have historically experienced an unemployment rate on average more than double that of skilled workers ("some college or above"). Furthermore, unskilled workers experience a higher risk of becoming unemployed during recessions and their unemployment rate is also more volatile (Mukoyama and Sahin 2006, p. 5 and note 1).

4 Some recipes to increase the social return of creative destruction

We believe that there are good reasons to hold that, in the last 40 years or so, unregulated processes of globalization and innovation have dramatically affected the balance between costs and benefits of creative destruction and their distribution within societies. In particular, internal and external deregulation and global competition have resulted in a race to the bottom in social standards: countries have been forced to reduce social safety nets and corporate taxation, thereby affecting their capability to redistribute income and finance social expenditure.

The mainstream economists argued that free movement of capital, goods, and people would lead to a more efficient allocation of resources and distribution of risk at the world level. Conversely, the empirical evidence suggests that deregulation and liberalization have brought about an inefficient redistribution of the costs of uncertainty within societies and on the global scale. Workers, and in particular the lower-skilled ones, are now less protected from unemployment and income risks, whereas entrepreneurs and top managers can more easily reduce the financial and real risks they face by exploiting diversification opportunities stemming from financial liberalization and the international delocalization of production. As a result, the business risk now carries more weight for the less educated and weaker social groups than it did 40 years or so ago.

The real benefits of a faster process of economic change through innovation are also debatable. Cannibalization among products and services is now the rule and the contribution of innovation to a better quality of life is often questionable.

In the previous chapters we discussed the impact of creative destruction on wellbeing, splitting economic change into its two basic components of shocks (in particular, but not only, technological progress) and policies (in particular, but not only, liberalization). Shocks and policies impacted wellbeing in different ways, exacerbating traditional problems such as the growing inequality and the economic cycle, or generating completely new problems, such as the COVID-19 pandemic recession and technological unemployment. The main result of our analysis is that the traditional approach greatly undervalues the negative impact of economic change on wellbeing. In fact, the mainstream economists disregard the psychological consequences of economic change, and hence its true cost, so that also their theoretical conclusions against the expediency of public intervention policies are inevitably biased.

DOI: 10.4324/9781003018230-5

Given these considerations, our opinion is that more active public policies are, in many circumstances, needed. The central idea is that the process of economic change should be publicly managed, but with the aim of minimizing its burden on the markets.

With a view to this goal, in the following sections, we discuss some policy recipes that may be implemented to reduce the costs imposed on the losers, redistribute the benefits and, by so doing, increase the social return of creative destruction. These policies may bring about a slowdown in the rate of creative destruction, but this outcome does not imply per se a slowdown in productivity growth. Rather, the opposite will hold if appropriate social accounting metrics are applied. Furthermore, the aim of these policies is to redirect technical change towards socially and environmentally sound goals rather than slowing it down.

Is there a reliable recipe to achieve sustainable economic change? Globalization and technical change have made the world more complex. Complexity requires ingenuity and creativity in policymaking. The behavioral and happiness economic principles (and tools) that we used to discuss the true cost of economic change bear important consequences, besides suggesting the expediency of public intervention, also on the choice of the policies to implement. In particular, building on D'Orlando and Ferrante (2008, 2009), and on D'Orlando, Ferrante and Ruiu (2011), we maintain that different policies can have different wellbeing consequences in different socioeconomic and cultural contexts. So, there is no one-size-fits-all approach to tackle specific problems: solutions should be sought on an eclectic basis. For example, liberalization policies can have good results in countries with a highly educated workforce, and poor results in countries with a poorly educated workforce. The pursuit of new models of social regulation is a venture similar to the one faced by low-income countries in their pursuit of an appropriate development strategy. On these grounds, an experimental and entrepreneurial approach should be adopted to discover the appropriate social arrangements (Hirschman 1958), i.e., microregulation and macroregulation policies that, relying on both markets and the state, can generate sustainable and inclusive economic growth in different cultural and social contexts (Rodrik 2007).

The interconnections among markets (labor, product, financial markets) and the interlinkages among sectors in the generation of economic change call for integrated policy packages inspired by the same goal: namely, to generate inclusive and sustainable economic growth and social progress. One of the advantages of an integrated policy package is that it can affect people's expectations and thereby generate a positive credibility outcome, enhancing its effectiveness. While the macroregulation policy is mainly needed to govern the natural tendency of the economic system to generate instability and uncertainty, microregulation policies are required to provide appropriate incentives to firms, workers, and consumers and to redistribute the rewards of creative destruction.

Most of the policy measures we discuss here are by no means new and simply need revising in the light of the new circumstances. Given the aim of this book, we will not offer a detailed and rigorous account of the different policy measures proposed but will focus mainly on the labor market, the market most affected by creative destruction. The OECD (OECD 2018a) provides a list of measures regarding education, the labor market, and the school-to-work transition, which are much in line with our approach.[1]

This chapter is organized as follows.

In Section 4.1, we focus on the labor market and recall both the negative consequences of economic change that we discussed in the previous chapters (unemployment, inequality, skills obsolescence, wage polarization, cyclical instability and recessions) and our conclusion that their impact on the general wellbeing is not homogenous among countries and more in general among social groups. As a consequence, if the objective of public intervention is the reduction of the wellbeing losses caused by economic change, the instruments to be used to achieve this result will vary greatly from one country to another and, furthermore, between the different social groups in the same country. Public intervention policy will therefore require complex policy mixes and no clear-cut solution for any single problem will be possible.

In Section 4.2, we summarize the results reached in the previous chapters (and sections) and sketch the foundations of the policy mix we propose.

In Section 4.3, we present our proposal regarding microregulation policies, mainly (albeit not solely) aiming at: (i) reducing the negative impact of loss aversion and incomplete hedonic adaptation process on those who have less in terms of skills and education; (ii) enhancing the ability of the less-skilled workers and/or workers undertaking routine tasks to resist technological displacement, thereby also counteracting inequality; and (iii) minimizing the spread and/or negative effects of populism. These policies consist of education policies, labor and industrial policies, antitrust and consumers' protection policies, reviewed in connection with the new scenario generated by globalization and on the basis of the robust empirical evidence provided by behavioral economics on cognitive biases.

In Section 4.4, we present our proposal regarding macroeconomic policies, mainly (albeit not solely) aiming at: (i) preventing the negative impact of the business cycle, recessions, and skill/task biased technical change on the general wellbeing by ex-ante counteracting the negative effects of such shocks on aggregate demand; (ii) counteracting the consequences of technological unemployment by using public subsidies to implement a universal basic income; and (iii) reducing the spread of economic crises and pandemics by limiting the movement of capital and/or people, or by indemnifying those hit by these crises. We first emphasize the new roles of fiscal policy in its different forms (in particular, public expenditure and subsidies); we then turn our attention to monetary policy, emphasizing the novelty consisting in its support for public expenditure in critical circumstance and its possible developments between two extremes, namely electronic money vs. sovereign money and the (new) Chicago Plan.

4.1 The labor market: different policies for different countries and social groups

In the previous chapters, we discussed both the causes and the consequences of economic change, emphasizing the greatly underrated role of psychological costs in determining the actual impact of the evolution of technology and of market regulations on people's wellbeing. When these costs are taken fully into consideration, the overoptimistic view holding that economic change implies always and only positive consequences appear theoretically and empirically weak. Of the many negative implications of economic change, we have discussed in particular the psychological consequences of its impact on workers and the labor market (although some sections have dwelt on other related themes) and the resulting (huge) negative impact on the general wellbeing. Public policies to manage technological progress in some way other than implementing liberalization policies, therefore, appear necessary, and indeed in most countries, they actually have been implemented.

However, different countries use different policy tools to meet the demand of the electoral body for protection against recessions, cyclical instability, unemployment, and more in general against the consequences of economic change. These tools mainly consist of social transfers, direct provision of public social services, and regulation of product and labor markets. All these policies are intrinsically redistributive, but their effects are quite different: social transfers and social public expenditure mainly redistribute income after it is produced, while labor and product market regulations, given their impact on labor demand and supply, lead to ex-ante redistributive effects. The specific mix of the three tools should be, and in reality often is, determined according to the actual demand for protection exerted by the electoral body.

Focusing on the labor market, and consistently with the aforementioned distinction, the main instruments used by policymakers around the world to counteract the effects of shocks on workers and the labor market are unemployment benefits (UB), Employment Protection Legislation (EPL), and Active Labour Market Policy (ALMP), in the specific form of training and retraining programs. The effects of the first two instruments are quite different: with employment protection legislation (i.e., job protection), the more strictly regulated labor markets show lower unemployment inflow and outflow rates, i.e., the frequency of unemployment episodes is lower but their duration longer; without employment protection legislation, but with unemployment benefits, less strictly regulated labor markets show higher unemployment inflow and outflow rates, i.e., the frequency of unemployment episodes is higher but their duration is shorter. As a result, stricter regulation reduces the probability of the less-skilled workers being fired but lengthens unemployment for all workers, including those with higher levels of education, who are less likely to lose their jobs anyway. The main implication is that the less regulated labor markets, which usually rely on unemployment benefits, improve the relative position of the workers with higher levels of education. On the contrary, more strictly regulated markets, which usually rely on employment protection legislations, improve the relative position of the workers with lower levels of education. The latter effect is produced, for a given unemployment rate u, by increasing unemployment duration d for both skilled and unskilled workers but leaving the unemployment frequency of skilled workers unaffected, i.e.,

$$u = d(f_s + f_{us})$$

$$d = \frac{u}{(f_s + f_{us})}; \quad \frac{\partial f_{us}}{\partial EPL} < 0; \frac{\partial f_s}{\partial EPL} \simeq 0 \tag{2}$$

where d and f are unemployment duration and frequency for, respectively skilled (s) and unskilled workers (us). Needless to say, there is a conflict of interest between workers with higher and lower levels of education that is regulated in the political market. In this respect, we should expect that the higher the ratio of high- to low-educated workers, the less the *EPL* will matter in the political equilibrium.

Avoiding any reference to the psychological costs of unemployment, and without referring to any specific cause for the phenomenon (i.e., independently of the circumstance that there is technological unemployment, or of the consequences of recessions, or of other causes), less strictly regulated labor markets and unemployment benefits thus seem the best choice for high-skilled workers and for countries with a higher percentage of them, whereas strict market regulation and employment protection legislation seem the best choice for low skilled workers and for countries with a higher percentage of them. But does anything change if we also take into consideration the psychological costs and their impact on wellbeing?

We know that the psychological costs of unemployment can hardly be offset by (monetary) unemployment benefits since, as pointed out in Chapter 3, the process of hedonic adaptation in the case of unemployment episodes is incomplete, preventing subjects from returning to the baseline level of wellbeing after a negative job-loss shock even after reemployment and therefore generating an irreversible wellbeing loss. Indeed, unemployment benefits are designed to compensate (at least partially) for the pecuniary losses stemming from joblessness, not to provide relief for these non-pecuniary losses. By contrast, job protection can reduce the nonpecuniary, psychological costs of unemployment by reducing the number of job-loss episodes that subjects face during their working life. The latter is a point of particular importance: the circumstance that each episode leaves the subject with an irreversible wellbeing loss implies that more frequent, short unemployment episodes generate a cumulative irreversible psychological loss greater than the psychological loss generated by fewer, even if longer, unemployment episodes. Therefore, repeated episodes of unemployment have a negative psychological impact that unemployment benefits are unable to remedy because the income that would be necessary to compensate people for the loss of wellbeing due to unemployment is very high: in Chapter 3 we saw that, according to many authors (see, e.g., Winkelmann and Winkelmann 1998; Frey and Stutzer 2002; Di Tella, MacCulloch and Oswald 2003), for a full compensation replacement ratio should be much greater than one.

As we pointed out in Chapter 3, the negative psychological impact of the previously described phenomenon is particularly relevant for fatalists and the lower-educated and less skilled, since they suffer greater wellbeing losses for each unemployment episode, and also suffer from more frequent unemployment episodes. They will consequently prefer employment protection legislation that reduces unemployment episodes rather than unemployment benefits which compensate only for the monetary but not the psychological costs of unemployment.

Therefore, nothing changes, compared to the conclusions we reached at the beginning of this section, if we also take into consideration the nonpecuniary costs of unemployment: the less-skilled workers, and the countries with a higher percentage of them, should prefer job protection (i.e., minimizing the number of unemployment episodes) to unemployment benefits (i.e., subsidizing the unemployed), as the empirical data confirm.[2]

However, strictly regulating the labor market is neither the only nor indeed the best policy intervention tool for reducing the number of unemployment episodes: these (workers and) countries might (call for and) implement policies, both at the microlevel and macrolevel, designed so as to ex-ante prevent exogenous shock from negatively impacting on the labor market, rather than policies aiming to regulate the labor market through employment protection legislation or indemnify those hit by the shocks. This is a fairly general conclusion that can apply to any cause of unemployment: business cycle, recessions, technological unemployment, etc. But in the case of rising unemployment caused by technological progress (i.e., technological unemployment) the subjective loss will be even greater since unemployment could prove permanent, and thus the demand for protection particularly urgent. Furthermore, this demand for protection will rise over time, as technological progress proceeds, and will rise in particular for those countries, or regions, specialized in productive processes highly intensive in low-skilled labor or particularly intensive in routine tasks. In these cases, the demand for protection will become impossible for the policymaker to resist, since it will be exerted by a growing share (and in the end by the majority) of the workforce.

The transitory phase, with rising unemployment, will be particularly problematic, since the skill (and/or task) segmentation of the labor market have a strong impact on the dynamics. If the labor market is segmented, the process of technological substitution of workers with machines (robots) will take place in successive steps. In a skill-biased technical change perspective, the process will first affect the unskilled workers, and only later the skilled workers, as technological progress spreads. Inequality will slowly increase, as well as the negative consequences for wellbeing caused by positional effects, and the demand for job protection will differ from region to region and country to country, with high-skilled countries demanding less protection than low-skilled countries. In a task-biased (or routine-replacing) technical change perspective the substitution will first affect workers performing routine tasks, and later workers performing nonroutine tasks, as technological progress spreads. In this case, it is not so easy to identify a priori which countries will require more protection, since we can find routine tasks in both low-skilled and high-skilled jobs (and countries). However, we will have a transition process that will take a long time and generate subsequent waves of unemployment for different categories of workers in different times and countries as innovations slowly spread in specific sectors or tasks. This dynamic process might generate subsequent waves of inequality among workers whose jobs require different skills, among workers whose jobs require routine or nonroutine tasks, and among workers living in different countries or regional areas (specialized in different jobs/tasks).

Managing such a complex process of creative destruction so as to minimize its impact on the general wellbeing is a challenging task, calling for a complex policy mix. In the following sections, we will extensively discuss some of the policies that may enter into this policy mix from both the microeconomic and macroeconomic perspectives.

4.2 The basis of our recipes

In particular, the policy mix we propose is based on the four main conclusions we have so far reached:

1 traditional theory is ill-equipped to correctly evaluate the true costs of economic change since it disregards the crucial importance of the psychological costs;
2 if the psychological costs are correctly computed, making use of some insights from behavioral economics, the economic change appears to affect different categories of subjects disproportionately, generating greater wellbeing losses for those who have less (in terms of skills and education);
3 these subjects (and those countries with a higher share of these subjects) will call for protection, and in particular, they will call for ex-ante intervention policies able to prevent unemployment rather than ex-post subsidies able to compensate them for their wage losses;
4 Over time the categories and the number of subjects hit by the economic change will rise (from unskilled workers to skilled workers, from workers performing routine tasks to workers performing also nonroutine tasks), as well as the demand for protection.

Policies have therefore to furnish flexible – and increasing over time – protection against wellbeing losses, and this protection should preferably consist in ex-ante policies aiming at preventing the impact of economic change on wellbeing, by either reducing the frequency and/or severity of the shocks caused by creative destruction or reducing the impact of these shocks on people's wellbeing. Strict market regulation policies and indemnifying policies acting after the shocks have impacted on wellbeing are also possible, but are far less efficient.

These policies require the application of microeconomic measures and/or macroeconomic measures to mitigate risks on an eclectic basis (Rodrik 2007; Hirschman 1958).

4.3 Changing incentives: microregulation revisited

The traditional economic theory supporting public intervention in the economy, and in particular the Keynesian approach, has often neglected the role of incentives and microregulation policy, relying almost exclusively on macroeconomic tools to manage aggregate demand. By microregulation policy, we mean all those measures implemented to regulate labor, product and financial markets and aiming to modify the incentive structure and redistribute the benefits of creative destruction. It is worth stressing here that behavioral economics provides strong empirical support for the idea that people's choices are affected by serious cognitive biases, and it offers insights into the way appropriate incentives should be tailored according to specific decisional contexts and cognitive biases.

In this book, we do not address the impact of different types of biases but limit our discussion to the main implications of loss aversion for policy design, and in particular for the labor market. An essential point to be stressed again is that the adoption of appropriate social accounting metrics is a necessary condition to assess the social return of any policy measure at both the macrolevel and microlevel.

Microregulation is a necessary complement of macroregulation within a more activist policy approach to economic change. In particular, microeconomic policies: (i) by raising subjects' levels of education, can successfully impact on fatalism and hence reduce the negative impact of loss aversion and incomplete hedonic adaptation on the less endowed (in terms of skills and education); (ii) by enhancing subjects' skill endowments, can help the less-skilled workers (and/or workers undertaking routine tasks) to resist technological displacement, thereby also counteracting inequality; finally, and (iii) by improving education and reducing income inequality could minimize the spread and/or the negative effects of populism.

Enhancing people's and societies' flexibility can increase the social return of economic change. Flexibility is not a normative issue, but rather a behavioral one. The more adaptable individuals will also be more prone to implement more flexible institutional settings, but the contrary may not hold, i.e., more flexible institutional settings may fail to lead to more flexible individuals. Populism is also the reaction of people to the attempt to force them to become flexible with a top-down approach based on deregulation. Leaving aside specific measures, education and training policy play a transversal, strategic role. People's capability to adapt to changing environments and to reap the benefits of economic change depends on their ability to deal with novelty and uncertainty. And knowledge and the skills acquired through education and training are essential tools to appreciate novelty (Di Giacinto and Ferrante 2007) and cope with uncertainty. Also, for this reason, education, training, and labor market policies should be seen as part of a coherent design that also includes industrial policy.

4.3.1 Enhancing people's flexibility: education, training, and labor market policy revisited

In Chapter 3, we recognized the key importance of *loss aversion* and *hedonic adaptation* in determining the cost of unemployment risk. Education, training, and labor market policies should be seen as part of the same policy package aiming at softening the impact of economic change on people's wellbeing by increasing their adaptability and thus reducing their sensitivity towards the two aforementioned behavioral principles. In this framework, labor market policy, together with industrial policy, should be addressed to regulate and accompany the process of reallocation of workers among firms and sectors. In Chapter 3, we also argued that the higher level of loss aversion and the consequent incompleteness of the hedonic adaptation process for the lower educated (low skilled) workers can have to do with underlying differences in culturally based beliefs (Guiso, Sapienza and Zingales 2006), and in particular different levels of *fatalism* and *trust in others*. And these traits are country-specific and culturally determined, so that people living in countries with a high share of fatalistic unskilled workers are more prone to call for, and rely on, employment protection legislation rather than, for example, unemployment benefits in unregulated markets. Our argument seems to be borne out by the fact that fatalism is a distinguishing feature of Southern European countries (Italy, France, Spain, and Portugal) and Japan, all countries which are characterized by the highest levels of employment protection legislation (D'Orlando, Ferrante and Ruiu 2011).

If we admit the possibility of a correlation between fatalism, loss aversion/ hedonic adaptation, and the levels of employment protection legislation of each country, to design policies aimed at reducing people's sensitivity towards loss aversion and hedonic adaptation it may be worth looking into why such heterogeneity among countries has arisen and persists. Indeed, this question is particularly relevant nowadays, when economic globalization and the growing role of *ICT* are held to have greatly contributed to the reduction of cultural heterogeneity among countries. The question can only be answered by scrutinizing the causes of the cultural dynamics, with particular regard to the incentives that people have in modifying their culture, beliefs, and institutional framework.

The incentive to modify a society's culture and values from inside depends on their comparative performance, i.e., on the extent to which, by adhering to them, most people get what they expect. Indeed, systematic frustration of people's expectations could start a lengthy process of cultural transformation, also leading to institutional change.[3] However, in general, a country's culture and beliefs modify slowly over time and, when modifications occur, there are major elements of irreversibility in the path of cultural and institutional evolution (North 1990). In this context, an important source of institutional inertia is a cultural transmission from old to young generations. Moreover, in some cases irreversibility interacts with random changes determining strong path dependence. In other words, two countries can initially share similar cultural characteristics, but they nonetheless can evolve towards two completely different cultural and institutional settings. The heterogeneity in the cultural framework of different countries which are, in other respects, quite similar, is thus a consequence of the past cultural and institutional evolution of these countries, and even if international economic integration and *ICT* allow for rapid dissemination of a unified culture throughout the world, the actual impact of this dissemination on a single country is slow and, interacting with that country's culture, may well generate a culture different to the one disseminated. This can also come about if the disseminating homogeneous cultural framework is consistent with institutions better suited to guaranteeing economic performance (North 1990): simply, the existing cultural framework may prevent people from recognizing the superiority of the disseminating culture and adopting it. Not to mention the case in which a cultural/institutional framework is shared by a majority of countries because it is fashionable or consistent with the interests of influential social actors, such as the entrepreneurs, but is not unambiguously more efficient than others and is thus rejected by a minority of countries.

In any case, the evolution of the cultural framework is not a completely exogenous process and policies may impact it. Among these policies, education plays a central role. People's preferences, values, and beliefs depend, over and above the effects of their socio-economic and cultural backgrounds, on the cognitive and noncognitive skills acquired early in life[4] through education and experience:

> Cognitive and noncognitive skills can affect the endowment of persons, their preferences, their technology of skill formation . . . or all three. Thus, they might affect risk preference, time preference, and efficiency of human capital productivity without necessarily being direct determinants of market wages.[5]
> (Heckman, Stixrud and Urzu 2006, p. 8)

Building on the latter conclusion, we should expect education to affect people's preferences, values, and beliefs through three main channels. First, it can modify– directly – the preferences, values, and beliefs of the young generations. Second, it can relax the responsiveness of individual preferences and beliefs to old values, enhancing people's self-determination.[6] Finally, education can modify people's responsiveness to different types of incentives by molding their motivations (Bowles, Gintis and Osborne 2001). The mitigating effect of education on the link between culture and beliefs/preferences (Guiso, Sapienza and Zingales 2006) helps explain why people in countries with higher levels of education show lower levels of fatalism, suffer less from loss aversion, adapt more easily to changes in occupational status and so call for less stringent *labor market regulation*.

The arguments developed offer guidance for policymakers concerning the efficiency and feasibility of reforms. First, policies that aim at increasing microeconomic flexibility should be primarily concerned with removing the causes of inflexible attitudes. Since the demand for job protection is negatively related to workers' skill levels, education and training policies may be powerful instruments to reduce the cost of economic change and the need for social protection. Education and training policy can do the job if inspired by the idea to provide all with equal opportunities to acquire the knowledge and skill needed to adapt to a fast-changing world. Inclusive education systems are the main goal that societies should pursue to obtain inclusive and sustainable economic growth.

The design of appropriate education systems and curricula is crucial. In a fast-changing environment, the best of worlds for employers would be one where (a) it is very easy to fire workers having obsolete skills and (b) firms can find workers possessing the specific skills to manage the new technology whenever needed, so there is no necessity to train new workers. Unfortunately, this is not the best of all possible worlds for workers and society at large, for they would have to bear the individual and social costs of this arrangement. The latter arrangement would rely heavily on schools and universities to provide workers with specific rather than general skills, thus limiting the chances of retraining workers when their human capital becomes obsolete. It goes without saying that, conversely, workers and society at large should be interested in employability over the workers' entire life cycle. Therefore, educational institutions should be more concerned with long-term rather than short-term worker employability, a solution that requires less specialized workers at entry into the labor market but that can be retrained over time. Of course, employers may not like it due to the training cost they have to bear when they hire new workers lacking the specific skills they need. Most important, *lack of internalization of workers' retraining costs by employers may provide biased incentives leading to a socially inefficient rate of creative destruction and worker turnover.*

The empirical evidence shows that (a) more inclusive education systems also show better learning outcomes and generate more inclusive social outcomes (OECD 2019) and (b) there is an employability trade-off concerning the distinction between general and specific skills. Educational curricula favoring advance professionalization, i.e., vocational education, rather than general education, appear to offer better opportunities of insertion at entry into the labor market at the cost of lower employability later in life (Hanushek et al. 2017). It follows that, in order to make people adaptable to changes in technology and demand for skills, educational systems should at all levels be designed to provide the right mix of general and professional education. In this context, the emphasis on STEM disciplines should not lead to neglecting the importance of humanistic studies in promoting people's ability to understand the world they live in.

In order to foster flexibility and reduce the subjective cost of economic change, school curricula should cultivate soft skills at all educational levels. In particular, entrepreneurial education can cultivate the proactive, problem-solving attitude needed to address uncertainty and novelty. To enhance creative and lateral thinking, teaching at secondary and tertiary levels should be based on principles of interdisciplinary contamination among STEM disciplines and liberal studies (Ferrante and Supino 2014; European Commission 2012). Within this approach, lifelong learning programs should be geared to adapt general skills to the contingent working needs generated by technical change.

Last but not least, according to the *cost disease* argument, the amount of resources that society channels into education should be assessed on the grounds that productivity in educational services cannot increase at the same rate as the other sectors (Baumol 1993). This could mean that to keep education quality at least constant increasing shares of GDP should be invested.

4.3.2 Industrial policy revisited: lessons from the Asian Miracle

Redistributing the gains from creative destruction and minimizing its negative impact on the wellbeing of those who have less should in any case not result in policies that reduce economic growth. On the contrary, greater redistribution requires greater growth. A feasible strategy to achieve this goal would appear to be a renewed approach to microregulation and, in particular, a revival of industrial and technology policy justified by the empirical evidence that it worked quite well in many developing countries (Cherif and Hasanov 2019; Andreoni, Chang and Scazzieri 2019). Economists have only recently started to recognize the fact that the rapid development seen by China, Singapore, Taiwan, etc. relied greatly on what can be defined nonorthodox strategic industrial policy. What we argue here is that the lesson to be learned applies not only to the developing countries but also to the developed ones in their attempt to govern and redirect the process of technical change in a sustainable way.[7]

Until the 1970s innovations contributed to solving people's basic problems and generated undoubted net social gains. This was essentially due to limited substitutability between old and new goods and services. Nowadays, many incremental innovations, due mainly to the diffusion of ICT, appear to offer society little benefit and have minor effects on productivity growth (Gordon 2012).

The idea that determination of the rate and direction of technical change should be left to the market forces contrasts with this outcome and with the evidence that they are unsustainable from the social and environmental point of view. The prevalence of giants in the marketplace like Amazon, Google, Apple, Microsoft, etc., controlling key technologies and large shares of their markets, suggests it is they that decide what game is to be played. So the choice for people is not between the *competitive market* and the government, as public choice theorists and free market economists would argue, but between the government and a few large corporations and financial institutions pursuing goals that, quite often, are in contrast with social ones. For instance, planned obsolescence of their products is a socially inefficient strategy followed by many corporations that should be opposed with appropriate measures at the national and international level. In many cases, consumers are induced by sophisticated marketing strategies or constrained by planned obsolescence to buy new versions of the products they use/consume which add only minor improvements. Such is the case with personal computers, smartphones, washing machines, etc. This is no new story (Scherer 1979), but the widespread diffusion of this practice in many industries is making it a deleterious social phenomenon, mainly because anticipated product obsolescence brings about anticipated depletion of physical and human capital within society and, consequently, potentially large efficiency losses:

> This strategy is profitable, because the quality of a new product is not immediately obvious and because firms can instill in the consumer the feeling that they need the newest version although the older one is still functioning well. There are hidden qualities which are not apparent until one has some experience with the product. Then there is a tendency to force consumers to switch by not providing compatibility with connectors or programs and not providing support indefinitely. Microsoft often forces upgrading by making older file versions inaccessible and inoperative.
>
> (Komlos 2014)

As far as the financial institutions are concerned, the Great Recession and inertia in reforming the financial sector have shown how distorted incentives are and how difficult it is to regulate finance due to lobbying and regulatory capture. The social benefits of innovative financial instruments and their contribution to people's wellbeing are often questionable (Zingales 2015). High private returns and low if not negative social rewards are often the outcome of financial innovations.

This state of affairs leaves room for public intervention in the form of industrial and technology policy, an idea that in the past was seen as practically anathema by pro-market economists and, in the 1990s, also staunchly opposed by the World Bank (Chang and Andreoni 2020).

Industrial policy has been defined either as an attempt by a government to encourage the movement of resources towards particular sectors that the government considers important for future economic growth (Krugman and Obstfeld 1991) or as policy favoring the more dynamic activities generally, regardless of whether they are located within industry or manufacturing (Rodrik 2004). Industrial policy was at the center of theoretical debate and actual implementation until the 1970s, the rationale for its implementation lying in coordination failure, dynamic scale economies, knowledge spillovers, and informational and environmental externalities, all circumstances capable of causing market failure and therefore requiring public intervention. Things changed at the end of the 1970s, when the idea that regulation of the rate and direction of technical change should be left to the market forces became fashionable and led to abandoning the debate on (and implementation of) industrial policy and, thus on the determinants of the direction of technical change. The theoretical bases in economics providing support to this latter view were grounded on the idea that markets work reasonably well and that any attempt to influence them would lead to inefficient outcomes: governments do not have better information than private agents on innovation opportunities and, in addition, they are less efficient than markets in allocating R&D expenditure. The only sector in which public intervention was accepted was antitrust policy and consumer protection. Starting from Ronald Reagan in the USA and Margaret Thatcher in the UK, policymakers embraced this view at different rates in different OECD countries. The conclusion that the government should not be interested in guiding the innovation processes also gave rise to the idea that industrial policy was not needed or could even be dangerous. The substantial renunciation of market regulation and, thus also the regulation of the rate and direction of technical change in order to reduce the social costs and redistribute the benefits of creative destruction is, in our view, the main cause of the present state of affairs. Luckily, the Great Recession contributed to reassessing the old view and legitimizing more public intervention. So it was that R&D and technology policy regained their centrality.

In this context, the understanding that technical change is a localized, path-dependent process (Atkinson and Stiglitz 1969; Acemoglu 2015), should take on a central role. The localized nature of technical change and the considerable inertia resulting from the cumulative nature of R&D brings about significant consequences and policy implications. Of the former, multiple equilibria and technological lock-in effects are the most important. Of the latter, coordinated policy measures may be required to escape from socially inefficient equilibria. To this end, microregulation policies are required. Specifically, industrial policy should factor in social and environmental sustainability goals. With a few exceptions, whereas the latter are often stressed in the official agendas of governments, the social impact and reward of innovation strategies and policies are often neglected. A new approach aiming to achieve sustainable economic change should be implemented by national governments and national and international agencies. The latter approach should be based, on one hand, on appropriate metrics to assess innovation projects and, on the other hand, on measures to avoid the deadweight costs of industrial crises and, by so doing, ease the process of reallocation of unemployed workers. Industrial policy should be part of a package including *social policies for innovation*, designed to support displaced people but also to ease the process of creative destruction. Public support should be provided on a universal basis and support programs should be implemented to help firms bear short-term financial disequilibria if they are economically viable. In this context, an appropriate mix of job protection also covering the self-employed and universal unemployment benefits should be adopted. The active market policy should be targeted to increasing employability, also through self-employment, mainly by means of lifelong learning programs.

In the case of publicly provided funds, the metrics of innovation benefits should give more weight to the social impact of innovations relative to their commercial viability and returns. Financial indicators included in the business plan, such as the net present value or the internal rate of return, should be based on this type of extended assessment. For instance, an estimate of the short-medium term impact on employment, the cost of retraining workers, and the cost imposed on the public budget to support the unemployed through social security schemes should be included in any private project aiming to achieve public support. This approach would also lead to the application of appropriate discount rates to take into account intergenerational distributional concerns.[8]

Measures leading innovators to internalize the social cost of creative destruction should be implemented, such as the duty for employers to provide workers with professional training at entry in the labor market as well as lifelong training. The high costs imposed on society by firms' strategies of planned/anticipated obsolescence should be dealt with at the national/international level through creative measures to avoid the risk of introducing inefficient barriers to innovation.

A critical perspective on open innovation, emphasizing its main drawbacks, is also needed. Open innovation is often referred to as a mechanism to make the process of innovation more inclusive and efficient. This is just one side of the coin. Open innovation strategies adopted by large corporations aim to externalize the innovative process in order to reduce *intra muros* investments in R&D to the minimum necessary to absorb knowledge externally generated and to reduce the risk borne: most of the costs and risks are borne mainly by millions of innovators/ start uppers on the global scale. R&D outsourcing, through open innovation, is simply the natural extension of the process of industrial outsourcing and fragmentation of international production experienced by the world economy in the last few decades. With open innovation, what the large corporations need to do is to manage the search process efficiently and pick the cherries when they are ripe, before their competitors do. Typically, the latter strategy is based on financing incubators and other mechanisms (Startup Academy, etc.) to scan the innovative ecosystems around the world. In such a way, most of the trial-and-error costs characterizing the innovation process are borne by thousands and thousands of start uppers and small firms around the world seeking fame and willing to accept a small reward for their ideas (although their ideas may be worth a lot for the large corporations). The balance sheet of the corporations that, finally, introduce the innovations does not include all these costs borne by the global innovation system. Leaving aside the distributive concern as to how the benefits of innovation are allocated within society, high private returns may well imply lower or even negative social reward of innovation efforts on the global scale. The dark side of open innovation is that it favors large corporations and leads to industrial concentrations in high-tech sectors within countries and on the global scale. There is robust evidence that the diffusion of open innovation has been followed by an increase of concentration in the control of technological assets, not to a reduction of it, as might have been expected. The cases of Apple, Google, and Amazon, whose market capitalization is equivalent to the GDP of some large countries, are perfect examples of the successful application of this strategy. This is surprising for a mechanism that should bring about more inclusive innovative processes and outcomes.

Widespread short-termism in people's decision-making, at all levels and in all circumstances, is the main cause of unsustainable processes of change. First, it is responsible for distorted incentive structures within firms. Performance-related pay schemes based on short-term targets, designed to generate dividends for shareholders, lead top managers to implement strategies bringing about short-term benefits rather than long-term ones. Cutting the wage bill or firing workers are two of the most efficient strategies to obtain such an outcome. Most importantly, due also to the separation between ownership and control, quite often top managers are able to design parachute contracts limiting their social responsibility. In this way, they do not internalize the costs of their strategies and mistakes – mistakes that may entail heavy costs for the workers, in particular if they are unskilled. More generally, the social costs of opportunistic behaviors and wrong managerial decisions increase with discretionary power, moving up within the firms' organization, and with the size of the firms. Entrepreneurs and top managers, in particular in large corporations, should be made more responsible for their choices and behaviors. The post-Great Recession period has clearly shown that the idea that self-regulation and the cultivation of managerial social responsibility would solve the problem is a mere illusion. Managerial social responsibility should be enforced through specific regulations binding contractual autonomy. Actually, the internalization of the social costs deriving from the exercise of managerial discretion would lead to more conservative strategies. But this is exactly their purpose.

Short-termism is particularly deleterious in the context of R&D investments. R&D policy should regain a long-term view in assessing the social returns of public funds. The increasing share of public money provided to support applied private research rather than university basic research and the shift in research funding away from the public sector towards private industry sources are the main determinants of short-termism in the appraisal of R&D projects, bringing about dynamic inefficiencies (Babina et al. 2020). Equally significant is the recent trend of national and international agencies to finance the private sector, universities, and research institutions on the basis of assessment of the commercial viability of their projects; it needs to be critically revised. The achievement of a high level of technology readiness (TRL), should not be considered a good predictor of the social merits of an innovative project. There is evidence that an approach to technology policy relying on commercial viability criteria is socially inefficient not only for the reasons discussed earlier but also due to the complementarity between the considerable knowledge spillovers from basic research and applied research[9] (Akcigit, Hanley and Serrano-Velarde 2017). Assessment of the quality of applied R&D projects borne by taxpayers should always include rigorous analysis of their social impact. In this context, social entrepreneurship[10] and social innovation should be accorded more room as tools to deliver goods and services in a sustainable way.

4.3.3 Antitrust and consumer protection policy

Another old-fashioned policy tool that deserves new attention and a slightly different focus is antitrust policy, which should be revised on at least two main grounds. First, the antitrust authorities should recognize that AI and the exploitation of big data have amplified the role of economies of scale and scope as market barriers and factors leading to the concentration of economic power.

The legacy of the contestable market approach (Baumol 1982) has also recently legitimized the idea that the size of the firms does not matter for competition and efficiency. Antitrust authorities have generally adopted this view. It is hard to think that size does not matter for the economy and society in the case of giants like Google, Amazon, etc. and that these companies are not able to react successfully to any attempt to threaten their abnormal profits. The steadily rising market capitalization of these companies is a clear sign that antitrust activity has been ineffective. The size of firms does not matter only for competition and the efficiency of markets. Being very big per se should be considered an overall threat for the economy, and indeed for the correct functioning of democracy. For the same reasons, even more dangerous is concentration in the financial markets. National antitrust agencies are not equipped to deal effectively with anticompetitive behaviors and supranational authorities should be created.

Second, antitrust activity should be designed taking into full account the evidence provided by behavioral economics on the fallacy of the idea that consumers are fully rational and, generally speaking, well informed. This does not mean that we back a paternalistic approach to the regulation of markets but that consumer sovereignty is a dangerous myth (Le Clair 2013). The continuous introduction of new goods and services with scant innovative content entails heavy learning costs and low social rewards, also because companies transfer onto them the rising costs of advertising expenditures needed to signal and amplify the perceived novelty content of goods. A large part of the investment behind the introduction of new goods and services consists of advertising costs. Not surprisingly, the data on advertising expenditure show a steadily increasing trend.[11] Paradoxically, in addition to generating barriers to entry, these investments increase the cost of learning to assess the intrinsic quality of the good instead of reducing it. Consumer protection legislation should tackle these common practices, which generate large distortions and also adversely affect market competition. Ingenuity and creativity in the choice of the appropriate policy tools are required to minimize the burden on genuine competition. Given that the information content of most advertising activity is very low, one might wonder whether the national fiscal agencies should limit the tax-deductibility of the advertising costs.

4.4 Back to the future: macroregulation policy revisited

Apart from microeconomic intervention policies, also macroeconomic stabilization policies can play a major role in counteracting the negative effects of creative destruction on the general wellbeing, at the same time boosting economic growth. These policies would in particular act by preventing the impact of shocks on the labor market, again in the logic that ex-ante prevention policies should in most cases be preferred to ex-post indemnification policies (and to strict market regulation), with the further and often neglected advantage of extending individuals' planning horizons thanks to the mitigation of uncertainty.

More in general, deficit spending and/or expansionary monetary policy, by raising aggregate demand and so production and employment, can prevent (or at least reduce) the negative impact of the business cycle, recessions, and skill/task biased technical change on subjects' employment status, wages and wellbeing, at the same time boosting investment, innovation, and economic growth; public subsidies can be used to counteract the monetary consequences of technological unemployment, for example by providing a universal basic income; public subsidies can also play a role in counteracting the effects of pandemics; controlling the movements of capital can reduce the spread of financial crises and the "race to the bottom" caused by unregulated globalization; etc.

The major candidates for these roles are, needless to say, fiscal and monetary policies.

4.4.1 Back to fiscal policy for full employment?

For our purposes, and to simplify a little, fiscal policy can be split into three main subcategories: changes in public expenditure, in transfer payments, and in taxation.

In the previous sections and chapters, we reached the conclusion that economic change generates both monetary and psychological losses for the weaker categories of society, and unemployment benefits can only compensate for monetary losses. We argued that this was the main reason why the weaker categories call for protection through more direct intervention tools than the mere provision of unemployment benefits. Therefore, as a general consideration, transfer payments (i.e., unemployment benefits) and taxation are to be considered in most cases, even if not useless, less useful than more direct intervention based on public expenditure and the direct supply of public services.

However, we have seen that different intervention policies are needed to cope with the needs of different social groups and countries, as well as (but this is a minor consideration) addressing single specific problems, so that the aforementioned consideration needs to be further specified for each concrete situation. For example, public subsides (i.e., transfer payments) can be used to counteract the negative effects of technological unemployment and pandemics, the general rule being that (strict market regulation and/or) indemnification policies are needed in the cases when prevention is impossible (or too costly in economic or social terms).

Focusing, as usual, on the labor market, our analysis led us to the conclusion that (i) stricter market regulation through employment protection legislations are useful for counteracting the negative psychological impact of unemployment on the less endowed (in skills and education), and can therefore have a role to play for countries with a high percentage of low-educated and low-skilled workers; and that (ii) less regulated markets and unemployment benefits can, by contrast, be more appropriate for countries with a high percentage of highly educated and high-skilled workers. However, stricter market regulations reduce economic efficiency and a country's competitiveness, so that different intervention policies appear in any case preferable. In particular, the government could use public expenditure to boost aggregate demand, production, and employment, so that neither the business cycle nor recessions raise unemployment, even without strict regulation of the labor market. In this way the government may avoid the negative impact of unemployment on the general wellbeing by counteracting the fall in aggregate demand that causes unemployment, acting in advance by preventing downturns, rather than simply forbidding layoffs, i.e. acting after downturns have come about and have negatively affected aggregate demand and labor demand. Indeed, the typical causal chain initiated by downturns (and recessions) runs as follows: (i) downturns, (ii) fall in aggregate demand, (iii) fall in labor demand, (iv) layoffs. Unemployment benefits come into play after the whole process has followed through; labor market regulation shortly before, avoiding layoffs; aggregate demand management through public expenditure comes into action before the whole process starts. The latter guarantees full employment, thereby minimizing the impact on the weaker subjects' wellbeing, without compromising competitiveness.

However, public expenditure has to be financed, and public finances in most countries have greatly suffered from the three twenty-first-century recessions (subprime, Eurozone, and COVID-19 crises). The result might be an untenable level of public debt. How can these intervention policies remain compatible with the sustainability of public finance? Furthermore, how can excessive indebtedness fare in the face of the Ricardo–Barro and Reinhart–Rogoff criticisms (see Section 1.1.2)?

The answer to these questions can be found in monetary rather than fiscal policy: even the mildest of the possible strategies for tackling the aforementioned problems, quantitative easing, ultimately requires the intervention of the Central Bank, which commits itself to buying public bonds. Other strategies will need stronger intervention tools, apparently unfeasible because they are inconsistent with the institutional framework, and statutes, of anti-inflationary, post-stagflation Central Banks. But the level reached by public debt with the pandemic has led economists to change their minds about what is feasible and what is unfeasible. In the next section, we will discuss the necessary monetary tools and resulting new role for monetary policy that emerged after the Covid-19 recessions. Therefore, a thorough discussion of the point (the ways to finance a rising public debt) is left to the next section.

Nonetheless, the idea of using public expenditure (and the resulting budget deficit) for preventing downturns and recessions, rather than using market regulations or unemployment benefits for offsetting the effects of downturns and recessions, can counteract the reduction in wellbeing caused by demand-side shocks, but will hardly be able to counteract the loss of wellbeing caused by supply-side shocks such as skill-biased technical change, task-biased technical change, and technological unemployment. Particularly problematic will be the transitory phases in which technological advances progressively affect certain tasks, generating increasing problems only for the workers engaged in these tasks. In all these cases different policies, and different policy mixes, can be preferable to increasing public expenditure, since boosting the demand for goods might result in an increase of labor demand only for certain tasks or only for robots, with no impact at all on the labor demand for workers whose jobs have been automated.

In these cases, direct intervention on the labor market might be unavoidable for at least two reasons: first, fired workers are likely not to obtain another job of the same quality; second, the concrete possibility that unemployment will not be temporary bears considerable psychological costs that dramatically reduce the fired workers' wellbeing. In these circumstances, unemployment benefits, including a universal basic income, cannot compensate for the psychological costs of layoffs and unemployment, while demand management policies are ineffective.

In the case of technological unemployment (but the reasoning can readily be extended to skill-biased and routine-replacing technical change) a mix of different policies might be the preferable option. One of these mixes is possibly combining payment of an unconditional basic income rising over time with Tietenberg's tradable permits approach (for a detailed description of this possible solution see D'Orlando 2020a, p. 11 and note xvii, D'Orlando 2020b, p. 612 ff., and D'Orlando 2021, section 4). With this approach, quotas of human employment are assigned to firms, which can in turn buy/sell their quotas to other firms, whereas human beings receive a subsistence allowance independent of whether they are employed or not. The strategy has three main advantages: first, firms can pay workers a wage below the subsistence bound given that in any case workers receive a public subsistence transfer, making human beings competitive with robots; second, firms or industries which find hiring human workers less profitable would sell quotas to firms or industries which have less disadvantage in employing human workers, so that human employment will concentrate where it hampers productivity least; third, a rising basic income mitigates the inability of monetary benefits to compensate for the non-pecuniary, psychological costs of unemployment caused by loss aversion (and might allow for linking the increase in the basic income to specific pro-social behaviors of individuals).

Finally, we must discuss the usefulness of policies aimed at regulating international movements of productive factors, such as capital and labor. These policies are usually claimed to be necessary for preventing the spread of financial crises, but also of the social problems associated with migration, and of pandemics. In these cases, too, our general rule seems to be valid: apart from the case of a pandemic, in which temporary limitations to the movement of people and the payment of subsidies to people negatively affected by the pandemic are unavoidable, free market strategies tempered by public expenditure to prevent the impact of crises on aggregate demand appear the best policy mix.

4.4.2 Chicago plan, helicopter money, e-money: the new role(s) of monetary policy

Monetary policy has greatly evolved over the last few decades, particularly subsequent to the subprime crisis. This evolution sped up during the European sovereign debts crisis and peaked with the COVID-19 pandemic: economic intervention policies that were once seen as mere theoretical speculation, and furthermore were at odds with the statutes of most Central Banks, have been reevaluated and considered perfectly feasible (and, moreover, in some cases have actually been implemented).

To better understand what has happened in the last twenty years, we must look back to the 1980s, when monetary policy saw another radical (and reverse) change, from a tool serving mainly to tackle unemployment and boost growth to a tool serving above all to tackle inflation. This change was a consequence of the mainstream theoretical dominance that affected economic theorizing in those years, together with the high inflationary rate and the failure of Keynesian intervention policies during the years of stagnation that followed the oil shocks. The main implication of the new (old, today) paradigm was the idea that monetary policy could only affect nominal magnitudes, and not real magnitudes, so that counteracting inflation was its only viable aim. The statutes of most Central Banks were modified accordingly, also bringing in rigid rules to prevent future Central Bankers from deviating from the new monetary orthodoxy. A side effect of the new approach was the idea that monetary policy was implemented better by modifying interest rates than the quantity of money, in accordance with the "Taylor rule."

As we suggested earlier, the twenty-first-century crises changed the aforementioned scenario, and the kind of policies that were actually implemented, although the Central Banks' statutes have remained unchanged. In particular, two converging dynamics affected monetary policy in the new century: the progressive revival of some old theoretical ideas in a new form, and the actual (emergency) imple-mentation of intervention programs capable of jeopardizing the traditional rigid separation between fiscal and monetary policy. As we show in the following, both these novelties can be linked in a single homogeneous design, even though their original inspiration is quite different.

The old theoretical ideas that are being revived today are the ones contained in the "Chicago Plan", proposed by Frank Knight, Henry Simons and other econo-mists in two versions in 1933, during the Great Depression (Knight 1933; Simons et al. 1933), summarized by Irving Fisher in 1936 (Fisher 1936), modified in 1939 (Douglas et al. 1939) and re-proposed in 2012 in a working paper by the Interna-tional Monetary Fund (Benes and Kumhof 2012).[12] Paradoxically, these ideas can also represent an answer to the challenge that electronic cryptocurrencies, such as the bitcoin, launched at Central Bank money (the paradox lying in the circum-stance that the philosophical basis of cryptocurrencies is diametrically opposite to the philosophical inspiration of the Chicago Plan).

The basic idea of the original plan, and its more recent versions, is that the commercial banks should limit their activities to lending the money previously received from someone else, and which they actually possess, playing only the traditional role of the intermediary that collects savings and passes them on to investors (in other words, complying with 100% backing of deposits by money). They should not create money ex nihilo, as they do today,[13] by issuing deposits when they grant loans. Such behavior, which can be induced with a variety of regulatory tools, implies that money can no longer be endogenously created by banks upon borrowers' demand. According to its proponents, under the Chicago Plan, there would be no more bank runs, and the public authorities would have better control of credit and thus of business cycle fluctuations.

The Chicago Plan evolved over time, but it remains the seminal contribution for the approach often called the "sovereign money" approach. It even ended up in a Swiss referendum proposal that was defeated on June 10, 2018.

The second converging process affecting monetary policy in the last two decades is the (partial) erosion of the traditional separation between monetary and fiscal policy. Starting from the sovereign debt crisis, but reaching practical implementation on a massive scale only during (and likely after) the COVID-19 pandemic, monetary policy took on the highly controversial role of financing public expenditure. The key tool to this end was the quantitative easing policy adopted by most Central Banks, which resembles, albeit with some important differences, the strategy of "helicopter money," as it is termed. We believe that, in the implementation of this strategy during the COVID-19 crisis, and furthermore in the proposals for its further implementation, quantitative easing strategies do not simply resemble helicopter money strategies, but are going to become indis-tinguishable from them, as borne out by the recent direct financing of govern-ments' expenses implemented by some Central Banks (e.g., the Bank of England).

Generally speaking, and although "exact definitions differ across the litera-ture, 'helicopter money', or 'money financing', broadly refers to a combina-tion of monetary and fiscal policies under which expansionary fiscal measures are financed by creating money rather than issuing debt" (Carter and Mendes 2020, p. 1).

Helicopter money was originally an idea of Milton Friedman (Friedman 1948), proposed to demonstrate that deflation was not a problem, since if it occurs a money drop "from the helicopters" will easily solve the problem. Therefore, according to Friedman's ideas, in their policy design, the Central Banks (and monetary policy) should focus on counteracting inflation, not deflation. To Friedman's way of thinking deflation was a rare and unlikely problem, so he was certainly not proposing the actual implementation of the instrument he created.

On the contrary, deflation and Great Recessions became a fairly frequent characteristic of the first two decades of the twenty-first century, so theoretical studies on the practical possibility of implementing a helicopter money strategy have multiplied. And, as we discuss in the following, the actual (current?) economic policies implemented by the Central Banks came close to such an outcome.

Apart from dropping it from helicopters, the simplest way of actually implementing Friedman's idea is to inject money into people's bank accounts so as to boost expenditure: in this way, monetary policy turns into transfer policy, i.e., one of the components of fiscal policy.

However, both dropping money from helicopters and wiring it (electronically, today) on bank accounts are not the actual way in which helicopter money has recently been theorized by the authors that developed its contemporary version.[14] According to them, with a helicopter money strategy the Central Bank could create (print) new digital money and use it directly to finance public expenditure without increasing the public debt (for example, by buying government bonds on the primary markets and immediately destroying these bonds), even if the possibility remains to directly finance the private sector by injecting digital money into private bank accounts, also in this case without generating new debt, or alternatively implement some similar strategies. The main characteristic of this policy is that the Central Bank finances a fiscal stimulus (either allowing higher public expenditure, or private spending) by *permanently* increasing the monetary base: the permanent nature of the monetary expansion being caused by the circumstance that the Central Bank increases its liabilities by expanding the monetary base without obtaining in exchange an equal quantity of salable assets, so that it will be unable to contract the monetary base in the future. The permanent nature of the policy also implies that subjects will not expect to be taxed to repay the fiscal stimulus (or will not expect to have to repay the loan) as is the case when public (or private) debt is issued in exchange for money, so they will not anticipate a reduction of their disposable permanent income and so will not reduce their consumptions, thus rendering the Ricardo–Barro argument irrelevant.

But is helicopter money really different from the contemporary strategies of quantitative easing, or asset purchase programs (APP), implemented by most Central Banks during the recent crises? And how relevant is the Ricardo–Barro argument in reality?

Prima facie the differences between quantitative easing/APP and helicopter money (in the version of acquiring public bonds and immediately destroying them, or suchlike) appear to be four in particular: (i) the aim of quantitative easing is the reduction of interest rates, whereas the main aim of helicopter money is financing public (or private) expenditure; (ii) under quantitative easing the increase in money supply is temporary, whereas under helicopter money it is permanent, so that the Ricardo–Barro argument is relevant only to the former; (iii) under quantitative easing the public debt rises, under helicopter money it remains unchanged, or even falls (if monetary financing is used to generate budget surpluses); (iv) under quantitative easing government bonds are acquired on the secondary market, under helicopter money they are acquired on the primary market.

Now, the aims of policies are certainly relevant, but what really matters are their results: if the results are the same, the policies cannot be considered significantly different. Furthermore, are we sure that the aim of quantitative easing is only reducing interest rates? For example, the Bank of England explicitly writes that "[t]he aim of QE is simple: by creating this 'new' money, we aim to boost spending and investment in the economy" (Bank of England 2020). Ultimately, today quantitative easing is used to indirectly finance government budget deficits, as helicopter money also aims to do. So it seems that the differences in the aims of the two tools do not matter so much. Second, under the quantitative easing strategies implemented by most Central Banks the rollover of public debt bonds acquired is usually explicitly guaranteed (i.e., Central Banks buy back new bonds from the government when the bonds they possess expire) so that the loan can be considered close to being irredeemable and thus the increase in money supply close to being permanent. In these circumstances, the only difference is that the commitment to a permanent rollover under quantitative easing can in the future be reversed, whereas under helicopter money this is impossible. However, after the COVID-19 pandemic crises some authors (Galì 2020; Giavazzi and Tabellini 2020) suggested that the Central Banks might buy irredeemable government bonds: now, since under quantitative easing the interest paid by governments on the bonds acquired by the Central Banks is usually paid back to the governments, implementing quantitative easing based on the acquiring of irredeemable bonds is actually indistinguishable from a helicopter money policy.[15] And in any case, the foundations of the Ricardo–Barro argument can be theoretically robust in a mainstream perfect information (or rational expectations) framework, but in the real world they inevitably appear weak, since it is hard to deny that subjects are almost always myopic. Finally, if the Central Bank buys irredeemable bonds it is true that these bonds are in any case public debt, but they are debt that will never be repaid: for all practical purposes, they cannot be considered as debt.

So the only significant difference between the two policies appears to be the fact that in one case the Central Bank acquires public bonds on the secondary market, and in the other on the primary market. Since in the end both the seller and the buyer are in the same situation, we believe that nothing serious changes if the acquiring procedure is carried out using intermediaries. Quantitative easing and helicopter money are therefore really very, very close.

It remains to discuss how this tendency of monetary policy to modify its goals by substituting the financing of public expenditure for price stability can fit in with the idea of sovereign money that we discussed previously. However, to address this point adequately we must first evaluate the challenge that digital currencies pose to the monetary role of the Central Banks and the possible reaction of these institutions to this challenge.

Indeed, the recent diffusion of cryptocurrencies represents a crucial challenge to the role of government-issued (fiat) money in the economic system and has the potential of substituting the current payment infrastructure with a completely different one. The most famous cryptocurrency is Bitcoin, which we can take to exemplify how this alternative payment infrastructure might work, and the problems it can generate. Bitcoin, with its blockchain architecture, is based on a decentralized accounting system within which anonymous transactions take place in electronic form using virtual money unconnected with Central Bank money. The total amount of Bitcoin is predetermined and cannot be changed, even if it has not yet been entirely supplied to the economy. And the residual amount not yet in circulation is relatively small. The supply of this residual small quantity of Bitcoin is managed by private subjects (factories, today), the miners, who produce Bitcoin by using huge computing power. With this supply process and the given total amount of the cryptocurrency, this system is rather similar to a system of payment based on gold: the quantity of gold existing in the world is given, but only a fraction of this given quantity has already been mined. The key point is that, because of the characteristics of the system described earlier, under such a payment infrastructure, discretionary and centralized variations in the quantity of money, and so policy strategies like quantitative easing and helicopter money, become impossible: the total amount of money is given, and residual increases in supply depend upon decentralized private initiative. The central banks risk losing one of their most powerful policy tools.

The problem is that the use of electronic payments, and so of virtual currencies, is an efficient and potentially costless system of payment alternative to cash, so that economic forces might easily cause a shift to the new system in the near future. According to Berentsen and Schar (2018, p. 101):

> [t]echnological reasons also apply: in the near future, a close cash substitute will be developed that will rapidly drive out cash as a means of payment. A contender is Bitcoin or some other cryptocurrency. While cryptocurrencies still have many drawbacks, such as high payment fees, scaling issues, and poor adoption, these issues could rapidly disappear with the emergence of large-scale off-chain payment networks (e.g., Bitcoin's lightning network) and other scaling solutions.

The problems described earlier, and the risk of development in the payment system that reduces the ability of the Central Banks to implement monetary policy, has forced Central Banks to study the possibility of issuing their own virtual (electronic) money. According to the scholars that have discussed the topic (see, e.g., Bordo and Levin 2017; Berentsen and Schar 2018), management of a system of payment based on sovereign digital currencies might be accomplished by allowing households and firms to "hold funds electronically in a digital currency account at the Central Bank. This digital currency will be legal tender for all payment transactions, public and private" (Bordo and Levin 2017, p. 2). Acting in this way the payment system will enjoy the advantages both of electronic means of payment and of allowing the Central Bank to manage monetary policy (in particular, changing money supply when necessary). Furthermore, the challenge represented by the possible diffusion of a decentralized and privately managed payment infrastructure would be addressed and the system would evolve in quite the opposite direction, i.e., towards a framework in which the monetary system would be much more centralized than it is now, with the possible loss of importance of private banks and an increase in the role and the importance of the Central Banks.

We can now put together all the elements described in this section and discuss how the new role of monetary policy (as a means for financing public expenditure) can fit in with the revival of the old idea of sovereign money. The last two decades have shown surprisingly fast evolution in the policy tools actually implemented by the Central Banks, and the theoretical debate is consistent with this evolution (even though in many cases actual implementation of policies has preceded thorough theoretical study): (i) quantitative easing has evolved towards a policy design that resembles helicopter money, with the monetary financing of government expenditure, and the possibility of implementing helicopter money in one of its pure and extreme forms is nowadays at the center of theoretical debate; (ii) the same theoretical debate has seen the resurgence of the ideas contained in the Chicago Plan, with the (not yet implemented) proposal of giving the Central Bank more rigid control over the money supply by limiting or eliminating the endogenous creation of money realized by commercial banks; finally, (iii) the development of cryptocurrencies and a decentralized system of payment potentially capable of crowding out cash has evolved in the opposite direction of projecting a centralized architecture in which the Central Banks issue electronic money and partially substitute the role played by the commercial banks in money supply.

All these points testify a strong evolution towards a greater role for the Central Banks and stronger control over money supply together with progressive reduction of the distance between monetary and fiscal policy.

In this evolving scenario, it appears possible to design a recipe for monetary-fiscal policies that combine sovereign money, electronic money, and helicopter money in a homogeneous policy mix capable of better counteracting both cyclical instability and recessions, preventing the impact of these events on aggregate demand, production, employment and thus on the general wellbeing. This policy recipe might be centered on the conjunction of three elements: (i) the possibility for private subjects to open accounts with the Central Bank; (ii) stricter control over commercial bank activities performed by the Central Bank under a sovereign money architecture; and (iii) implementation of the most typical form of helicopter money, i.e., boosting consumption with the direct injection of fresh money into the bank accounts of citizens. In such a scenario the injection of money would be performed directly on the electronic accounts held by households and firms at the Central Bank. This policy would be complementary, and not alternative, to the direct monetary financing of public expenditure, reaching the double result of financing both consumption and public expenditure.

The policy mix suggested would achieve a number of results: (i) allowing Governments to implement the fiscal expansion required by great recessions also in a situation of high public debt – and in particular, allowing governments to implement the policies we proposed in the previous section; (ii) boosting consumption; (iii) guaranteeing a permanent increase in money supply capable of positive impact on inflationary expectations; (iv) reducing economic instability; (v) preventing bank runs; (vi) simplifying payments through the use of electronic money; (vii) macroregulating the economy (and reducing the negative impact of shocks on wellbeing) without interfering in the free functioning of the product and labor markets, i.e., safeguarding economic efficiency.

Needless to say, the statutes of most Central Banks should be modified in accordance with the new approach to the monetary policy described earlier.

Finally, the recipe we propose would also contribute to solving the main problem faced by economic policy nowadays, namely the difficulty of implementing monetary policy at the zero lower bound. The idea is widely accepted that nominal interest rates cannot fall below zero, or can fall below zero only for a very small amount. So if the recovery of an economy requires negative real interest rates, as is usually the case in a liquidity trap or a secular stagnation scenario, the Central Banks come up against great difficulties in driving the actual real interest rate towards its equilibrium level, in particular in the presence of low inflationary expectations.[16] Thus, monetary policy loses its main intervention tool, i.e., management of the interest rate. It should therefore leave room for fiscal policy to boost aggregate demand, income, and employment. But fiscal policy is bounded by the high level of public debt reached in many countries. Direct monetary financing of consumption and public expenditure would be capable of allowing aggregate demand to rise, restoring full employment.

It is certainly true that the permanent increase in the quantity of money can raise price levels and, if repeated, inflation. But inflation is exactly what we need today. If it will become an issue tomorrow, in the scenario we depicted the possibility will remain for central banks to counteract the increase in prices (not by selling assets but) by eliminating the endogenous creation of money realized by commercial banks.

4.4.3 Fighting tax havens and fiscal dumping

Tax havens and fiscal dumping are two deleterious phenomena responsible for the race to the bottom in social standards and increasing difficulties in financing national welfare systems:

> Tax havens collectively cost governments between $500 billion and $600 billion a year in lost corporate tax revenue, depending on the estimate (Crivelli, de Mooij and Keen 2015; Cobham and Janský 2018), through legal and not-so-legal means. Of that lost revenue, low-income economies account

for some $200 billion – a larger hit as a percentage of GDP than advanced economies and more than the $150 billion or so they receive each year in foreign development assistance. American Fortune 500 companies alone held an estimated $2.6 trillion offshore in 2017 [. . .]. Corporations aren't the only beneficiaries. Individuals have stashed $8.7 trillion in tax havens, estimates Gabriel Zucman (2017), an economist at the University of California at Berkeley. Economist and lawyer James S. Henry's (2016) more comprehensive estimates yield an astonishing total of up to $36 trillion. Both, assuming very different rates of return, put global individual income tax losses at around $200 billion a year, which must be added to the corporate total.

(Shaxson 2019)

Fiscal dumping is equally deleterious for national welfare systems. For instance, Munoz (2019) shows that fiscal competition within a political union can generate a welfare loss of 20% for the bottom 50% of the population, where the benchmark is federalism without tax competition.

In the past, fiscal competition coupled with free capital movements has been advocated as an efficiency-enhancing mechanism. Conversely, the data on increasing inequality and lower social mobility show that in an "imperfect world" it reduces the redistributive capability of the state and favors a race to the bottom in social standards. It goes without saying that taking actions that should be implemented through multilateral agreements to fight tax havens and limit fiscal competition is a policy priority for all governments willing to credibly embrace the SDG Agenda of the World Bank.

Notes

1 "First, education measures to support social mobility and to avoid unequal opportunities in the long run include access to high-quality early education and care, as well as formal education for all, while preventing school drop-out. Second, public investment in health has the potential to support social mobility over the life course and across generations, for example by cushioning income losses or necessary labor market changes when health issues arise. A strategy based on greater investment in children targeting those from lower socio-economic backgrounds holds the promise of breaking the cycle of intergenerational disadvantages. In particular, access to sickness insurance for all households is a prerequisite. Third, family policies, in particular policies that promote a good work and family balance, early education and care policies and services, can help level the playing fields for all children by compensating disadvantages at home and avoiding the transmission of disadvantages to children. They can also support parents in their participation to the labor market and mitigate the detrimental impacts of financial hardship on children's future outcomes. Fourth, policies affecting wealth accumulation and savings behavior are an important tool for enhancing social mobility. Avenues to rebalance opportunities would be to limit wealth, inheritance and gifts tax avoidance, design progressive tax systems with adequate rates and reduce exemptions. Finally, fostering social mobility also requires policies to reduce regional divides and spatial segregation in cities. This necessitates a range of well-coordinated local development and urban planning policies including measures for transport and housing, such as inclusionary zoning policies. First, income-support schemes for the unemployed, set at an adequate

level associated with active labor market policies and re-training strategies can help cushion the negative impact of life events for individuals from disadvantaged background but also for their offspring, with positive spillovers in non-income areas. Second, labor market policies which strengthen the transition from school to work, address occupational barriers for disadvantaged groups, or ensure that recruitment processes are fair, can make a substantial difference for earnings and occupational mobility throughout the career of disadvantaged workers" (OECD 2018a, p. 19).

2 See, e.g., D'Orlando and Ferrante (2009, pp. 106–107). Indeed, the empirical data seem to confirm that the lower educated workers suffer lower rates of unemployment in the more regulated labor markets (about half that of the less regulated countries), so we may conclude that job protection legislation is an effective means of redistributing occupational opportunities among workers with different educational attainments.

3 For example, people may realize that, in the face of labor market flexibility, markets do not generate equal opportunities. Or, conversely, that labor market regulation yields more job insecurity than expected due to very long unemployment spells.

4 The socio-economic outcomes that appear to depend on these cognitive abilities include: educational achievement, occupational status, income, delinquency and criminal behavior, poverty, divorce, having an illegitimate child, being on welfare, having an underweight baby, etc.

5 The supporting empirical evidence on the effect of cognitive and non-cognitive skills on an individual life is impressive. As far as cognitive skills are concerned, the list of individual characteristics correlated with the standard measurement tests is indeed long, ranging over: abilities (analytical style, memory, reaction time, reading), creativity (craftwork, musical ability), health and fitness, interests (breadth and depth of interests, sports participation), morality (delinquency, lie scores, racial prejudice, values), perceptual elements (ability to perceive brief stimuli, field-independence, myopia), personality (achievement motivation, altruism, dogmatism) and practical skills (practical knowledge, social skills).

6 Lower educated societies are, as might be expected, based on more stable cultural values and a weaker role for individual self-determination (e.g., agricultural vs. industrial societies).

7 This point is supported by Mazzucato's analysis (Mazzucato 2013), which shows that in the USA, too, public funds for R&D are a major ingredient of successful innovations.

8 Indeed, this type of assessment is very demanding. As in the case of financial projections in standard business planning, the aim of this assessment is not rigorous computation of these costs but comparison of alternative options in terms of social impact and making the different stakeholders aware of the importance of this impact.

9 "Our key finding is that standard innovation policies (e.g., uniform R&D tax credits) can accentuate the dynamic misallocation in the economy by oversubsidizing applied research. Policies geared towards public basic research and its transmission to the private sector are significantly welfare improving" (Akcigit, Hanley and Serrano-Velarde 2017, p. 2)

10 "It is the entrepreneurship that has as main goal to address pressing social challenges and meet social needs in an innovative way while serving the general interest and common good for the benefit of the community. In a nutshell, social entrepreneurship targets to social impact primarily rather than profit maximisation in their effort to reach the most vulnerable groups and to contribute to inclusive and sustainable growth" (www.oecd.org/cfe/leed/social-entrepreneurship-oecd-ec.htm).

11 For example, www.statista.com/statistics/269964/global-advertising-expenditure-by-region/.

12 For a thorough description of the history of the Chicago Plan see Benes and Kumhof (2012, pp. 17–19).

13 "[U]nder the present system banks do not have to wait for depositors to appear and make funds available before they can on-lend, or intermediate, those funds. Rather, they create their own funds, deposits, in the act of lending" (Benes and Kumhof 2012, p. 9).

14 The main contemporary contributions on the theme of helicopter money are by Bernanke (2002, 2003, 2016), Woodford (2012), Buiter (2014), Turner (2013, 2015), Bartsch et al. (2019), Galí (2019).

15 Apart from the possibility of the Central Bank selling these bonds to the private sector: in this case interest will not return to the Government.

16 The actual real (expected) interest rate that drives investment decisions is given by the nominal interest rate, controlled by the Central Bank, minus the (expected) inflation rate. If the nominal interest rate has already reached its lower bound, i.e. zero or a little below zero, the only possibility for the Central Bank to drive the actual real interest rate toward the negative level that would realize full employment is by increasing inflationary expectations.

5 Conclusions
Looking for sustainable economic change

Economic debate on the determinants of the rate and direction of technical change was very much in vogue in the 1960s and the 1970s. The theory of induced innovation was the main analytical tool developed in this context and, in simple terms, it was based on the idea that the rate and direction of technical change is determined by resource scarcity, as signaled by the price system, and by opportunities to innovate in the various directions (Ahmad 1966; Nordhaus 1973). In this context, there was also room for industrial policy motivated by market failures generating inefficient price signals. The idea that regulation of the rate and direction of technical change should be left to the market forces, with no room for governments, came into vogue at the end of the 1970s. The theoretical bases supporting this view were provided by the neoclassical counterrevolution and were grounded on the idea that markets work reasonably well in conveying information about people's needs. In addition, governments were assumed to have no better information than private agents on innovation opportunities and to be less efficient than markets in allocating R&D expenditure.

Leaving aside the more recent consequences, i.e., the Great Recessions, the long-term effects of that view are now quite clear. Environmental crises, escalating inequality, reduced social mobility, increasing social and economic fragility are all evidence that the world we live in is not a better one for a lot of people. In particular, the increase in social and economic immobility bears critical consequences:

> Increasingly, an individual's chances in life are determined by their starting point (socio-economic status at birth, where they were born, etc.), resulting in economies and societies that all too often reproduce rather than reduce historic inequalities. Across most socio-economic systems today a person's background often predetermines the level of education they will attain, the type of work they will do and the level of income they will earn. This "lock-in" from birth has consequences for growth, cohesion and innovation across societies.
> (WEF 2020, p. 8)

Furthermore, institutions at all territorial levels are now weaker in addressing the complexity of the world and ill-equipped to address the global challenges.

DOI: 10.4324/9781003018230-6

Populism and nationalism are irrational people's reactions to the frustration deriving from the inability of politics to cope with this complexity.

Among the main failures of the *rhetoric of economic growth without regret*, on which policymaking in OECD has been based in the last 40 years or so, is failure to recognize a major feature of the human mind, namely loss aversion. People's asymmetric assessment of gains and losses should lead to revising the trade-off between economic growth and macroeconomic stability, which conventionally assigns to the former a very high priority in policymaking. Widespread loss aversion calls for institution design based on a different priority, mitigation of all the risks to which people are now exposed, including health risks. We are not suggesting here that countries should give up economic growth; rather, we believe that it is feasible to combine economic growth with sustainable development – sustainable in its comprehensive sense, not simply environmental but also social and in terms of wellbeing. So, the issue is not to stop growing but to redirect economic growth.

To achieve this goal the role played by the institutions is crucial, since formal and informal institutions are fundamental determinants of the socio-economic performance of countries:

> Institutions are the rules of the game in society or, more formally, are the humanly devised constraints that shape human interaction. In consequence they structure incentives in human exchange, whether political, social, or economic. The purpose of the rules is to define the way the game is played. But the objective of the team within that set of rules is to win the game.
>
> (North 1990)

In our view, the game that has not been played in the last forty years or so and should be played is one leading to inclusive and wellbeing-enhancing economic growth. Accordingly, we define as a sustainable social arrangement an institutional regime that can generate such an outcome by influencing the process of creative destruction, or in other words the rate and direction of technical change.

The global pandemic has re-proposed in dramatic terms the fundamental role of governments in managing crises and mitigating health and economic risks, highlighting the effects generated by the weakening of the role of governments, especially in the field of health and social security. It is no coincidence that, of the most advanced countries, those that have withstood the impact of the pandemic least are those where the role of the state is weaker, such as the USA and the UK.

In Section 4 of this book, we discussed some of the main policy measures that can be implemented to achieve the goal, stressing their specific objectives rather than their technical features. In a complex and interdependent world, policymakers should be aware that there is no *one size fits all approach* to sustainable and inclusive economic change. The choice of the appropriate social arrangement should emerge through an experimental process of search and entrepreneurial discovery of the best solution.

Inclusive economic growth requires short-term losers in the process of change to be supported by society and the benefits of change redistributed. This choice does not necessarily imply that private incentives to innovate will prove too weak if the public authorities provide appropriate support to R&D innovative projects, all of which offer positive social impacts. Adoption of this approach will eventually have a positive impact on technical progress and its social return, by redirecting it towards social goals. In this context, the target of fostering social mobility is a priority:

> The economic and social returns from investing in the right mix of social mobility factors are substantial. If countries included in this report were to increase their social mobility index score by 10 points, this would result in an additional GDP growth of 4.41% by 2030 in addition to vast social cohesion benefits.
>
> (WEF 2020)

Maintenance of social, human, and environmental capital should be considered a guiding principle inspiring any policy. This goal should be pursued through wide-ranging interconnected policy measures based on the adoption of appropriate metrics of the costs of economic change, which should include its social, human capital, and environmental impacts, i.e. assessment of its impact on the depletion of the stock of the three forms of capital. Fighting financial short-termism in the assessment of the social returns of economic activity is another priority that should inform any policy measure. In the latter respect, a major benefit of macroeconomic management policy is the broadening of individuals' and societies' planning horizons obtained through the mitigation of uncertainty.

Institutions are characterized by considerable inertia. The adoption of an encompassing and integrated policy package, including education, industrial, social, and labor market policies, is essential for dealing with this inertia and enhancing the effectiveness and political feasibility of individual measures.

Implementation of inclusive education systems is the keystone of this approach since education can reduce the subjective cost of economic change and support a more inclusive process of economic growth by enhancing equal opportunity in the labor market. In order to make people adaptable to changes in technology and demand for skills, educational systems at all levels should be designed to provide the right mix of general and professional education. In order to foster flexibility and reduce the subjective cost of economic change, school curricula should at all levels include modules of entrepreneurial education and should be based, at secondary and tertiary levels, on principles of interdisciplinary contamination. Entrepreneurial education can cultivate the proactive, problem-solving aptitude needed to cope with the new developments while interdisciplinary contamination can enhance creativity and the ability to find new solutions.

In addition to microregulation policies, macroeconomic management policies are required to smooth economic fluctuations and thereby mitigate risk, also in consideration of people's loss aversion. In particular, when shocks are particularly strong monetary policy could be given the role of financing not only Government budget deficit, but also private consumption and investment (by bringing in some form of helicopter money). The government should add public expenditure to these private expenses, thus boosting aggregate demand, production, and employment, so that neither the business cycle nor recessions would aggravate unemployment, even without a great deal of labor market regulation. In this way, the government prevents negative wellbeing shocks by counteracting the fall in aggregate demand that causes unemployment and wage reduction. The general rule is that ex-ante policies aiming to prevent the impact of the negative consequences of creative destruction on the general wellbeing are preferable to ex-post policies designed to indemnify the losers, although, for particular phenomena, such as technological unemployment, different policy mixes might be preferable.

The race to the bottom in social standards experienced in the last few decades is the inevitable destiny of an unregulated process of global competition where competition prevails over cooperation. Reform of national policies should therefore be complemented by a new approach to international relationships based on a revival of multilateralism and the creation of the supranational institutions needed to deal with a complex and interdependent world.

Within a sustainable social arrangement, the role of the political institutions should not be underestimated. The inability of politics to pursue long-term social goals and tackle global issues is the other side of the coin of a process of economic change characterized by increasing inequality. In the past, public choice theorists and free market economists have emphasized the risks of regulatory capture due to excessive public intervention. After 40 years of deregulation, governments are now very weak in the face of corporations with a market capitalization equivalent to the GDP of a developed country, such as Apple or Amazon.[1] Major investment funds can also put pressure on governments in their attempts to regulate global financial markets. Therefore, and paradoxically, regulatory capture is far more likely today, in the presence of too little public intervention, than in the past, testifying that the problem had been correctly understood but the solution had not.

On the other hand, the Internet and the diffusion of social media have not helped to enhance democratic control over governments – quite the opposite. Populism is the wrong answer to the right question, due also to the quality of information available on the social media. Like finance,[2] populism is fostering short-termism in the political agenda.

Democratic institutions are under serious threat due to pressure from powerful economic and financial lobbies and inadequate democratic control. We need an overall rethinking of democratic systems taking into account the technological, social, and cultural transformations that have occurred in the last 40 years or so.

5.1 Towards a behavioral economic theory of the long run

The standard approach to market-driven economic change is based on a Promethean optimism that was justified until a few decades ago by the ample benefits brought about by technological and scientific advances in the 20th century. We are now aware that the process of creative destruction, through which economic change proceeds, may not deliver generalized improvements in wellbeing when basic needs have already been satisfied and people's major life problems solved.

The empirical evidence on the relationship between happiness and per capita income growth bears out the conclusion that economic growth may fail to bring about higher levels of subjective wellbeing in developed countries: the income elasticity of happiness and life satisfaction may prove quite low.[3]

Leaving aside the consequences of market failures and the distributional impact of an unregulated process of creative destruction, the main and most important methodological error, at the origin of the standard approach to economic change (Lucas 2003), is the idea that people evaluate gains and losses in the same way. Behavioral economics and the evidence on loss aversion suggest this is not the case. In this book, we have discussed the implications of this idea in the context of the labor market. More generally, policymakers should be aware that the preference for the status quo due to loss aversion is an innate psychological trait, characterizing the vast majority of people and decision settings, and should design policies in accordance with this conclusion.

Given loss aversion, economic policy, i.e., macroregulation and microregulation policies, should factor in that people are not so willing to trade off their familiar standard of living for an uncertain prospect of a better one in the future, as envisaged by the free market economists.

Regret aversion is another reason to reappraise the conventional wisdom about the benefits of innovation. Expanding choices through the introduction of new goods and services is a good thing but the psychological costs should not be disregarded, in particular whenever their novelty content is low.

Piecing all these elements together, we can summarize our conclusions on the relation between long-term economic change (i.e., growth) and people's wellbeing as follows:

1   Traditional (mainstream) theory strongly emphasizes the positive consequences of technological progress, economic change, and creative destruction for the economy as a whole and for all social categories, including the less endowed (in terms of skills and education).

2   However, we maintain that traditional theory not only disregards some of the main negative consequences of technological progress (e.g., technological unemployment), but in particular cannot adequately assess the true costs of the whole process of creative destruction since it disregards the crucial importance of psychological costs, and in particular loss aversion.

3   As a result, a traditional theory greatly undervalues the negative effects of economic change on the wellbeing of both the less endowed and the economy as a whole.

4   Once correctly evaluated, the costs may be seen to be greater than the gains for the economy as a whole, as is almost certainly the case with the less endowed.

5   The aforementioned considerations might induce people to call for more protection against economic change by throwing themselves behind populist movements attempting to stop the process.

6 The success of these movements risks indiscriminately suppressing both the positive and negative consequences of creative destruction, generating even more social costs.

7 Actually, policies capable of combining the positive outcomes of creative destruction with reduction of its negative consequences do exist.

8 As a general rule, policies designed to prevent the impact of the negative consequences of creative destruction on the general wellbeing are preferable to ex-post policies indemnifying the losers in the process (even if, for particular phenomena, e.g., technological unemployment, different policy mixes might be preferable).

9 These policies combine the free functioning of most markets, ensuring economic efficiency, with both microeconomic and macroeconomic intervention strategies.

10 Microeconomic regulation policies aim mainly (though not solely) at ex-ante mitigation of the negative impact of loss aversion and skill/task polarization, in particular by supporting new and different education policies.

11 Macroeconomic stabilization policies combine the new roles of monetary policy (e.g., financing public expenditure and supporting private expenditure) with government public intervention to forestall the impact of economic shocks resulting from an economic change on people's wellbeing.

12 If we take into serious consideration, as indeed we should, the cost disease argument, we should allocate increasing shares of resources to health and education (Baumol 1993).

Finally, one may wonder whether it is politically feasible to combine long-term economic growth, induced by creative destruction, with the safeguarding of people's long-term wellbeing. Indeed, the ample role we assign to governments should be complemented with greater accountability on the part of politicians and public action: market and nonmarket failures are equally deleterious for a society's welfare. In any case, we maintain that there are no alternatives to this type of *new deal* in economic policy. Disregarding the true costs of economic change will, as it did in the 1930s, jeopardize the future of mankind mainly by boosting the influence of the populist and nationalist parties.

Notes

1 The market capitalization of Apple and Amazon in 2020 reached respectively, 2,200 and 1,700 billion dollars (www.macrotrends.net/stocks/charts/AMZN/amazon/market-cap).
2 For a clear description of how finance can easily degenerate into a rent-seeking activity, see, e.g., Zingales (2015).
3 On the debate on this point see, e.g., Easterlin (2001, 2013).

References

Acemoglu, D. (2015). "Localised and Biased Technologies: Atkinson and Stiglitz's New View, Induced Innovations, and Directed Technological Change", *Economic Journal*,125(583), pp. 443–463

Acemoglu, D. and Autor, D. (2011). "Skills, Tasks and Technologies: Implications for Employment and Earnings", in *Handbook of Labor Economics*, edited by D. Card and O. Ashenfelter, Vol. 4, Part B, pp. 1043–1171, North Holland, San Diego, CA

Acemoglu, D. and Restrepo, P. (2016). "The Race Between Machines and Humans: Implications for Growth, Factors Shares and Jobs", https://voxeu.org/article/job-race-machines-versus-humans

Acemoglu, D. and Restrepo, P. (2017). "Robots and Jobs: Evidence from US Labor Market", *NBER Working PaperNo. 23285*, www.nber.org/papers/w23285, https://doi.org/10.3386/w23285

Acemoglu, D. and Restrepo, P. (2019). "Automation and New Tasks: How Technology Displaces and Reinstates Labor", *Journal of Economic Perspectives*, 33(2), pp. 3–30

Acemoglu, D. and Robinson, J. (2002). "The Political Economy of the Kuznets Curve", *Review of Development Economics*, 6(2), pp. 183–203

Agell, J. (1999). "On the Benefits from Rigid Labor Markets: Norms, Market Failures, and Social Insurance", *Economic Journal*, 109(453), pp. 143–164

Aghion, P., Akcigit, U., Deaton, A. and Roulet, A. (2016). "Creative Destruction and Subjective Well-Being", *American Economic Review*, 106(12), pp. 3869–3897

Aghion, P. and Bolton, P. (1997). "A Theory of Trickle-Down Growth and Development", *The Review of Economic Studies*, 64(2), pp. 151–172

Aghion, P., Caroli, E. and Garcìa-Peñalosa, C. (1999). "Inequality and Economic Growth: The Perspective of the New Growth Theories", *Journal of Economic Literature*, 37(4), pp. 1615–1660

Ahmad, S. (1966). "On the Theory of Induced Invention", *Economic Journal*, 76, pp. 344–357

Akcigit, U., Hanley, D. and Serrano-Velarde, N. (2017). "Back to Basics: Basic Research Spillovers, Innovation Policy and Growth", *National Bureau of Economic Research, Working Paper No. 19473.* https://www.nber.org/papers/w19473

Akcigit, U. and Sina, T.A. (2019). "Ten Facts on Declining Business Dynamism and Lessons from Endogenous Growth Theory", *National Bureau of Economic Research, Working Paper 25755.* https://www.nber.org/papers/w25755

Alesina, A. and Ardagna, S. (2009). "Large Changes in Fiscal Policy: Taxes Versus Spending", *National Bureau of Economic Research, Working Paper No. 15438.* https://www.nber.org/papers/w15438

Alesina, A. and Perotti, R. (1994). "The Political Economy of Growth: A Critical Survey of the Recent Literature", *The World Bank Economic Review*, 8(3), pp. 351–371, www.jstor.org/stable/3989954

Alesina, A. and Perotti, R. (1996). "Income Distribution, Political Instability, and Investment", *European Economic Review*, 40, pp. 1203–1228

Alesina, A. and Rodrik, D. (1994). "Distributive Politics and Economic Growth", *The Quarterly Journal of Economics*, 109(2), pp. 465–490, www.jstor.org/stable/2118470

Allen, J. and van der Velden, R. (2001). "Educational Mismatches Versus Skill Mismatches: Effects on Wages, Jobsatisfaction, and On-the-job Search", *Oxford Economic Papers*, 3, pp. 434–452

Alm, S. (2011). "Downward Social Mobility across Generations: The Role of Parental Mobility and Education", *Sociological Research on Line*, 16(3), pp. 1–14

Alvaredo, F., Chancel, L., Saez, E., Zucman, G. and Piketty, T. (2017). *World Inequality Report*, World Inequality Lab. https://wir2018.wid.world/files/download/wir2018-full-report-english.pdf

Anders, G. (1956). *Die Antiquiertheit des Menschen. Über die SeeleimZeitalter der zweiteninindustriellen Revolution*, C.H. Beck, München

Andreoni, A., Chang, H. and Scazzieri, R. (2019). "Industrial Policy in Context: Building Blocks for an Integrated and Comparative Political Economy Agenda", *Structural Change and Economic Dynamics*, 48, pp. 1–6

Arrow, K. and Debreu, G. (1954). "Existence of an Equilibrium for a Competitive Economy", *Econometrica*, 22(3), pp. 265–290, https://doi.org/10.2307/1907353.

Atkinson, A.B. and Stiglitz, J.E. (1969). "A New View of Technological Change", *Economic Journal*, 79, pp. 573–578

Aubert, N. (2003). *Le culte de l'urgence. La société malade du temps*, Flammarion, Paris

Autor, D.H. and Dorn, D. (2013). "The Growth of Low-Skill Service Jobs and the Polarization of the US Labor Market", *American Economic Review*, 103(5), pp. 1553–1597

Autor, D.H., Goldin, C. and Katz, L. (2020). "Extending the Race between Education and Technology", *AEA Papers and Proceedings*, 110, pp. 347–351

Autor, D.H. and Handel, M. (2013). "Putting Tasks to the Test: Human Capital, Job Tasks, and Wages", *Journal of Labor Economics*, 31(2), pp. 59–96

Autor, D.H. and Katz, L. (1999). "Changes in the Wage Structure and Earnings Inequality", in *Handbook of Labor Economics*, edited by O. Ashenfelter and D. Card, Vol. 3A, pp. 1463–1555, Elsevier Science B.V., Amsterdam

Autor, D.H., Katz, L. and Kearney, M. (2006). "The Polarization of U.S. Labor Market", *American Economic Review*, 96(2), pp. 189–194

Autor, D.H., Katz, L. and Kearney, M. (2008). "Trends in U.S. Wage Inequality: Revising the Revisionists", *Review of Economics and Statistics*, 90(2), pp. 300–323

Autor, D.H., Katz, L. and Krueger, A. (1998). "Computing Inequality: Have Computers Changed the Labor Market?", *Quarterly Journal of Economics*, 113(4), pp. 1169–1214

Autor, D.H., Levy, F. and Murnane, R.J. (2003). "The Skill Content of Recent Technological Change: An Empirical Exploration", *Quarterly Journal of Economics*, 118(4), pp. 1279–1333

Azariadis, C. (1975). "Implicit Contracts and Underemployment Equilibria", *Journal of Political Economy*, 83(6), pp. 183–1202

Babina, T., Xi He, A., Howell, S.T., Perlman, E.R. and Staudt, J. (2020). "The Color of Money: Federal vs. Industry Funding of University Research", *National Bureau of Economic Research, Working Paper No. 28160.* https://www.nber.org/system/files/working_papers/w28160/w28160.pdf

Baily, M. (1974). "Wages and Employment Under Uncertain Demand", *Review of Economic Studies*, 41, pp. 37–50

Baldwin, R. (2006). "Globalisation: The Great Unbundling(s)", *Economic Council of Finland*, 20(3), pp. 5–47

Banerjee, A. and Newman, A. (1993). "Occupational Choice and the Process of Development", *Journal of Political Economy*, 101(2), pp. 274–298

Bank of England (2020). "What Is Quantitative Easing?", www.bankofengland.co.uk/monetary-policy/quantitative-easing

Bartolini, S., Bilancini, E. and Pugno, M. (2013). "Did the Decline in Social Connections Depress Americans' Happiness?", *Social Indicators Research*, 110, pp. 1033–1059

Bartsch, E., Boivin, J., Fischer, S. and Hildebrand, P. (2019). "Dealing with the Next Downturn: From Unconventional Monetary Policy to Unprecedented Policy Coordination", *Macro and Market Perspectives* (August), BlackRock Investment Institute

Bauman, Z. (2000). *Liquid Modernity*, Polity, Cambridge

Bauman, Z. (2003). *Liquid Love: On the Frailty of Human Bonds*, Blackwell, Oxford

Baumol, W.J. (1982). "Contestable Markets: An Uprising in the Theory of Industry Structure", *American Economic Review*, 72(1), pp. 1–15

Baumol, W.J. (1993). "Health Care, Education and the Cost Disease: A Looming Crisis for Public Choice", in *The Next Twenty-five Years of Public Choice*, edited by C.K. Rowley, F. Schneider and R.D. Tollison, Springer, Dordrecht

Beck, U. (1986). *Risikogesellschaft. Auf dem Weg in eineandereModerne, Suhrkamp Verlag, Frankfurt am Main; Risk Society: Towards a New Modernity*, Sage, London, 1992

Benabou, R. and Ok, E. (2001). "Social Mobility and the Demand for Redistribution: The Poum Hypothesis", *The Quarterly Journal of Economics*, 116(2), May, pp. 447–487, https://doi.org/10.1162/00335530151144078

Benes, J. and Kumhof, M. (2012). "The Chicago Plan Revisited", *IMF Working PaperWP/12/202*, www.imf.org/external/pubs/ft/wp/2012/wp12202.pdf

Berentsen, A. and Schar, F. (2018). "The Case for Central Bank Electronic Money and the Non-case for Central Bank Cryptocurrencies", *Federal Reserve Bank of St. Louis Review*, Second Quarter 2018, pp. 97–106, https://doi.org/10.20955/r.2018.97-106

Berg, A., Buffie, E. and Zanna, L. (2018). "Should We Fear the Robot Revolution? (The Correct Answer is Yes)", *Journal of Monetary Economics*, 97(C), pp. 117–148

Bernanke, B.S. (2002). "Deflation: Making Sure 'It' Doesn't Happen Here", Remarks before the National Economists Club, Washington, DC, November 21

Bernanke, B.S. (2003). "Some Thoughts on Monetary Policy in Japan", Remarks before the Japan Society of Monetary Economics, Tokyo, Japan, May 31

Bernanke, B.S. (2016). "What Tools Does the Fed Have Left? Part 3: Helicopter Money", *Brookings Institution Blog*, April 11. B. https://www.brookings.edu/blog/ben-bernanke/2016/04/11/what-tools-does-the-fed-have-left-part-3-helicopter-money/

Bertola, G. and Rogerson, R. (1997). "Institutions and Labor Reallocation", *European Economic Review*, 41(6), pp. 1147–1171

Bessen, J. (2018). "AI and Jobs: The Role of Demand", *National Bureau of Economic Research, Working Paper 24235*. https://www.nber.org/papers/w24235

Bhanumurthy, N. and Mitra, A. (2004). "Declining Poverty in India: A Decomposition Analysis", *Institute of Economic Growth Discussion Paper*, Delhi University, Enclave, Delhi, www.iegindia.org/workpap/wp248.pdf

Blanchard, O. and Landier, A. (2001). "The Perverse Effects of Partial Labor Market Reform: Fixed Duration Contracts in France", *National Bureau of Economic Research, Working Paper 8219*. https://www.nber.org/system/files/working_papers/w8219/w8219.pdf

Blien, U. and Ludewig, O. (2017). "Technological Progress and (Un)employment Development", *IZA Discussion PaperNo. 10472*, http://ftp.iza.org/dp10472.pdf

Boeri, T. and Garibaldi, P. (2007). "Two Tier Reforms of Employment Protection: A Honeymoon Effect?", *The Economic Journal*, 117(521), pp. 357–385, https://doi.org/10.1111/j.1468-0297.2007.02060.x

Bordo, M. and Levin, A. (2017). "Central Bank Digital Currency and the Future of Monetary Policy", *Hoover Institution Economic Working Papers*, Economics Working Paper 17104, www.hoover.org/sites/default/files/research/docs/17104-bordo-levin_updated.pdf

Bowles, S., Gintis, H. and Osborne, M. (2001). "The Determinants of Earnings: A Behavioral Approach", *Journal of Economic Literature*, 39(4), pp. 1137–1176

Brinca, P., Duarte, J.B. and Faria-e-Castro, M. (2020). "Is the COVID-19 Pandemic a Supply or a Demand Shock?", *Economic Synopses*, n. 31(2020), pp. 1–3

Brunello, G., Garibaldi, P. and Wasmer, E. (2007). *Education and Training in Europe*, Fondazione Rodolfo De Benedetti, Oxford University Press, Oxford.

Brynjolfsson, E. and McAfee, A. (2011). *Race Against the Machine*, Digital Frontier Press, Lexington, MA.

Brynjolfsson, E. and McAfee, A. (2014). *The Second Machine Age*, W. W. Norton & Company, New York, NY and London.

Buchanan, J.M. and Tullock, G. (1962). *The Calculus of Consent: Logical Foundations for Constitutional Democracy*, The University of Michigan Press, Michigan.

Buiter, W.H. (2014). "The Simple Analytics of Helicopter Money: Why It Works – Always", *Economics, The Open-Access, Open-Assessment E-Journal*, n. 8(2014–28), pp. 1–45.

Bukodi, E., Goldthorpe, J.H., Waller, L. and Kuha, J. (2015). "The Mobility Problem in Britain: New Findings from the Analysis of Birth Cohort Data", *British Journal of Sociology*, pp. 66, 93–117.

Calvino, F. and Virgillito, M.E. (2018). "The Innovation-Employment Nexus: A Critical Survey of Theory and Empirics", *Journal of Economic Surveys*, 32(1), pp. 83–117

Campa, R. (2017). "Technological Unemployment. A Brief History of an Idea", *ISA eSymposium for Sociology*, pp. 1–16, www.academia.edu/31689849/Technological_Unemployment

Card, D. and DiNardo, J. (2002). "Skill-biased Technical Change and Rising Wage Inequality: Some Problems and Puzzles", *Journal of Labor Economics*, 20(4), pp. 733–783

Carter, T. and Mendes, R. (2020). "The Power of Helicopter Money Revisited: A New Keynesian Perspective", *Bank of Canada Staff Discussion Paper/Document d'analyse du personnel2020–01*, www.bankofcanada.ca/wp-content/uploads/2020/02/sdp2020-1.pdf

Chang, H. and Andreaoni, A. (2020). *Industrial Policy in a Changing World. Basic Principles, Neglected Issues and New Challenges*. Wiley online Library, https://doi.org/10.1111/dech.12570

Chaudhuri, A. (1985). "Formal Properties of Interpersonal Envy", *Theory and Decision*, 18(3), pp. 301–312

Cherif, R. and Hasanov, F. (2019). "The Return of the Policy That Shall Not Be Named: Principles of Industrial Policy", *IMF WP/19/74*. https://www.imf.org/en/Publications/WP/Issues/2019/03/26/The-Return-of-the-Policy-That-Shall-Not-Be-Named-Principles-of-Industrial-Policy-46710

Chetty, R., Grusky, D., Hell, M., Hendren, N., Manduca, R. and Narang, J. (2017). "The Fading American Dream: Trends in Absolute Income Mobility Since 1940", *Science*, 2017 Apr 28, https://scholar.harvard.edu/files/hendren/files/abs_mobility_paper.pdf

Cialdini, R. (2006). *The Psychology of Persuasion*, Harper Business

Clark, A.E., Georgellis, Y., Lucas, R.E. and Deiner, E. (2002). "Unemployment Alters the Set-Point for Life Satisfaction", mimeo, https://citeseerx.ist.psu.edu/viewdoc/download?doi=10.1.1.524.9658&rep=rep1&type=pdf

Clark, A.E., Georgellis, Y., Lucas, R.E. and Diener, E. (2004). "Unemployment Alters the Set-Point for Life Satisfaction", *Psychological Science*, 15(1), pp. 8–13

Clark, A.E., Georgellis, Y. and Sanfey, P. (2001). "Scarring: The Psychological Impact of Past Unemployment Experience", *Economica*, 68, pp. 221–241

Clark, A.E. and Oswald, A.J. (1994). "Happiness and Unemployment", *Economic Journal*, 104(424), pp. 648–659

Combes, P., Magnac, T. and Robin, J. (2004). "The Dynamics of Local Employment in France", *Journal of Urban Economics*, 56, pp. 217–243

Corak, M. (2013). "Income Inequality, Equality of Opportunity, and Intergenerational Mobility", *Journal of Economic Perspectives*, 27(3), pp. 79–102

Corry, D. (1996). *Economics and European Union Migration Policies*, Institute for Public Policy Research, London

Cunha, F. and Heckman, J. (2007). "The Technology of Skill Formation", *American Economic Review*, 97(2), pp. 31–47

De Neve, J.-E., Ward, G.W., De Keulenaer, F., Van Landeghem, B., Kavetsos, G. and Norton, M.I. (2015). "The Asymmetric Experience of Positive and Negative Economic Growth: Global Evidence Using Subjective Wellbeing Data", *Centre for Economic Performance (CEP) Discussion Paper no. 1304.* https://cep.lse.ac.uk/pubs/download/dp1304.pdf

Di Giacinto, M. and Ferrante, F. (2007). "Idiosyncratic Learning, Creative Consumption and Well Being", *Advances in New Austrian Economics*, 10, pp. 41–73

Di Tella, R., Haisken-De New, J. and MacCulloch, R. (2007). "Happiness Adaptation to Income and to Status in an Individual Panel", *National Bureau of Economic Research, Working Paper 13159.* https://www.nber.org/papers/w13159

Di Tella, R., MacCulloch, R. and Oswald, A. (2001). "Preferences over Inflation and Unemployment: Evidence from Surveys of Happiness", *American Economic Review*, 91(1), pp. 335–341

Di Tella, R., MacCulloch, R. and Oswald, A. (2003). "The Macroeconomics of Happiness", *Review of Economics and Statistics*, 85(4), pp. 809–827

Dolan, P. and Lordan, G. (2013). "Moving Up and Sliding Down: An Empirical Assessment of the Effect of Social Mobility on Subjective Wellbeing", *CEP Discussion Papers* (CEPDP1190), Centre for Economic Performance, London School of Economics and Political Science, London, UK

Dollar, D., &Kraay, A. (2002). "Growth Is Good for the Poor", *Journal of Economic Growth*, 7(3), pp. 195–225, www.jstor.org/stable/40216063

Dolmas, J. (1998). "Risk Preferences and the Welfare cost of the Business Cycle", *Review of Economic Dynamics*, 1(3), pp. 646–676

D'Orlando, F. (2020a). "Technological Unemployment and the Resurgence of Political Economy", *American Review of Political Economy*, 15(1), pp. 1–25, https://doi.org/10.38024/arpe.of.6.28.20

D'Orlando, F. (2020b). "On Technological Unemployment", *La Comunità Internazionale*, fasc. 4(2020), pp. 593–623

D'Orlando, F. (2021). "Social Interaction, Envy, and the Basic Income: Do Remedies to Technological Unemployment Reduce Well-being?", *Basic Income Studies*, Forthcoming

D'Orlando, F. and Ferrante, F. (2008). "Why Do Similar Countries Have Different Labour Market Regulations?", *La Comunità Internazionale*, LXII(1), pp. 61–76

D'Orlando, F. and Ferrante, F. (2009). "The Demand for Job Protection. Some Clues from Behavioral Economics", *Journal of Socio-Economics*, 38(1), pp. 104–114

D'Orlando, F. and Ferrante, F. (2018). "Macroeconomic Priorities Revisited: The Behavioural Foundations of Stabilization Policies", *Cambridge Journal of Economics*, 42(5), pp. 1255–1275, https://doi.org/10.1093/cje/bex076

D'Orlando, F., Ferrante, F. and Ruiu, G. (2011). "Culturally Based Beliefs and Labor Market Institutions", *Journal of Socio-Economics*, 40(2), 150–162

D'Orlando, F. and Ricciotti, S. (2021). "The Economics of Escalation", *Rationality and Society*, 33(1), pp. 106–140, https://doi.org/10.1177/1043463120985310

D'Orlando, F. and Sanfilippo, E. (2010). "Behavioral Foundations for the Keynesian Consumption Function", *Journal of Economic Psychology*, 31(6), December, pp. 1035–1046

Douglas, P., Fisher, I., Graham, F., Hamilton, E., King, W. and Whittlesey, C. (1939). "A Program for Monetary Reform", revisedAProgramforMo#A7DF1B.doc (chicagobooth.edu)

Dunlop, J. (1944). *Wage Determination under Trade Unionism*, Macmillan, New York

Durkheim, E. (1893). *De la divisiondutravail social. Félix Alcan, Paris; The Division of Labour in Society*, Routledge and Kegan Paul, London, 1982

Dustmann, C., Ludsteck, J. and Schönberg, U. (2009). "Revisiting the German Wage Structure", *The Quarterly Journal of Economics*, 124(2), pp. 843–881

Easterlin, R.A. (2001). "Income and Happiness: Towards a Unified Theory", *Economic Journal*, 111(473), pp. 465–484

Easterlin, R.A. (2004). "Explaining Happiness", *Proceedings of the National Academy of Sciences*, 100(19), 1176–1183

Easterlin, R.A. (2013). "Happiness and Economic Growth. The Evidence", *IZA Discussion Papern. 7178.* http://ftp.iza.org/dp7187.pdf

Ehrenberg, A. (1995). *L'individuincertain*, Calmann-Lévy, Paris

Epstein, L. and Zin, S. (1991). "Substitution, Risk Aversion, and the Temporal Behaviour of Consumption and Asset Returns: An Empirical Analysis", *Journal of Political Economy*, 99(2), pp. 263–286.

European Commission (2012). "Effects and Impact of Entrepreneurship Programs in Higher Education", *DG Enterprise and Industry*, Brussels

Fagereng, A., Guiso, L., Malacrino, D. and Pistaferri, L. (2020). "Heterogeneity and Pesistence in Returns to Wealth", *Econometrica*, 88(1), pp. 115–170

Feldmann, H. (2013). "Technological Unemployment in Industrial Countries", *Journal of Evolutionary Economics*, 23(5), pp. 1099–1126.

Fernandez, R. and Rodrik, D. (1991). "Resistance to Reform: Status Quo Bias in the Presence of Individual-Specific Uncertainty", *American Economic Review*, 81(5), pp. 1146–1155

Fernández-Macías, E. and Hurley, J. (2016). "Routine-biased Technical Change and Job Polarisation in Europe", *Socio-Economic Review*, 15(3), pp. 565–585

Ferrante, F. (2009). "Education, Aspirations and Life Satisfaction", *Kyklos*, 62(4), pp. 542–562

Ferrante, F., McGuinness, S. and Sloane, P.J. (2010). "Esiste 'Overeducation'? Un'analisi Comparata", in (a cura di) *Consorzio Interuniversitario AlmaLaurea. XII Rapporto sulla condizione occupazionale dei laureati. Investimenti in capitale umano nel futuro di Italia ed Europa*, pp. 73–115, Il Mulino

Ferrante, F. and Supino, S. (2014). "Le misure di sostegno alla nuova imprenditorialità. Le buone pratiche su scala europea, con particolare riferimento all'educazione imprenditoriale [SupportingEarly-stage Entrepreneurship]", *MPRA Paper68930*, University Library of Munich, Germany

Festinger, L. (1957). *A Theory of Cognitive Dissonance*, Stanford University Press, Stanford, CA

Fischer, P.A., Martin, R. and Straubhaar, T. (1997). "Should I Stay or Should I Go? International Migration, Immobility and Development", in *Internationa Migration, Immobility and Development: Multidisciplinary Perspectives*, edited by T. Hammer, G. Brochmann, K. Tamas and T.Faist, Berg Publishers, Oxford

Fisher, I. (1936). "100% Money and the Public Debt", *Economic Forum*, Spring Number, April–June 1936, pp. 406–420

Fitoussi, J.-P., Jestaz, D., Phepls, E.S. and Zoega, G. (2000). "Root of the Recent Recoveries: Labor Reforms or Private Sector Forces?", in *Brooking Papers on Economic Activity* (1), pp. 237–291

Ford, M. (2015). *Rise of the Robots: Technology and the Threat of a Jobless Future*, Basic Books, New York, NY

Fornaro, L. and Wolf, M. (2020). "Covid-19 Coronavirus and Macroeconomic Policy", *Barcelona GSE, Working Paper 1168*.

Frank, R.H. (2005). "Positional Externalities Cause Large and Preventable Welfare Losses", *American Economic Review*, 95(2), pp. 137–141

Freeman, R. (2005). "Labor Market Institutions without Blinders: The Debate Over Flexibility and Labor Market Performance", *National Bureau of Economic Research, Working Paper 11286*. https://www.nber.org/papers/w11286

Freeman, R. (2015). "Who Owns the Robots Rules the World", *IZA World of Labor*, https://wol.iza.org/articles/who-owns-the-robots-rules-the-world/long

Frey, B. and Stutzer, A. (2002). "What Can Economists Learn from Happiness Research?", *Journal of Economic Literature*, XL, June, pp. 402–435

Friedman, M. (1948). "A Monetary and Fiscal Framework for Economic Stability", *The American Economic Review*, 38, June, pp. 245–264

Friedman, M. (1957). *A Theory of the Consumption Function*, Princeton University Press, Princeton

Galí, J. (2019). "The Effects of a Money-Financed Fiscal Stimulus", *Journal of Monetary Economics*, 105, pp. 21–43

Galí, J. (2020). "Helicopter Money: The Time is Now", *Voxeu*, https://voxeu.org/article/helicopter-money-time-now

Galor, O. and Zeira, J. (1993). "Income Distribution and Macroeconomics", *Review of Economic Studies*, 60(1), pp. 35–52

Garibaldi, P. (1998). "Job Flows Dynamics and Firing Restrictions", *European Economic Review*, 42(2), pp. 245–275

Giavazzi, F. and Pagano, M. (1990). "Can Severe Fiscal Contractions be Expansionary? Tales of Two Small European Countries", *NBER Macroeconomics Annual*, 5, pp. 75–111

Giavazzi, F. and Pagano, M. (1996). "Non-Keynesian Effects of Fiscal Policy Changes: International Evidence and the Swedish Experience", *Swedish Economic Policy Review*, May, pp. 75–111

Giavazzi, F. and Tabellini, G. (2020). "Covid Perpetual Eurobonds: Jointly Guaranteed and Supported by the ECB", *Voxeu.org*, https://voxeu.org/article/covid-perpetual-eurobonds

Goldin, C. and Katz, L.F. (2009). *The Race between Education and Technology*, Harvard University Press, Cambridge, MA

Goos, M. and Manning, A. (2007). "Lousy and Lovely Jobs: The Rising Polarization of Work in Britain", *The Review of Economics and Statistics*, 89, pp. 118–133, https://doi.org/10.1162/rest.89.1.118

Goos, M., Manning, A. and Salomons, A. (2014). "Explaining Job Polarization: Routine-Biased Technological Change and Offshoring", *American Economic Review*, 104(8), pp. 2509–2526

Gordon, R. (2012). "Is U.S. Economic Growth Over? Faltering Innovation Confronts the Six Headwinds", *National Bureau of Economic Research, Working Paper 18315*. https://www.nber.org/papers/w18315

Gregory, T., Salomons, A. and Zierahn, U. (2019). "Racing with or Against Machine? Evidence from Europe", *IZA Working Paper 12063*. https://www.econstor.eu/bitstream/10419/193357/1/dp12063.pdf

Grolleau, G., Mzoughi, N. and Sutan, A. (2006). "Do You Envy Others Competitively or Destructively? An Experimental and Survey Investigation", https://ssrn.com/abstract=930103 or http://dx.doi.org/10.2139/ssrn.930103

Guerrieri, V., Lorenzoni, G., Straub, L. and Werning, I. (2020). "Macroeconomic Implications of COVID-19: Can Negative Supply Shocks Cause Demand Shortages?", *National Bureau of Economic Research, Working Paper 26918*. https://www.nber.org/papers/w26918

Guiso, L., Jappelli, T. and Pistaferri, L. (1999). "An Empirical Analysis of Earnings and Unemployment Risk", *CSEF Working Paper*, Università di Salerno n. 8

Guiso, L., Sapienza, P. and Zingales, L. (2006). "Does Culture Affect Economic Outcomes?", *Journal of Economic Perspectives*, 20(2), pp. 23–48

Gupta, S. and Choudhry, N.K. (1997). "Globalization, Growth and Sustainability: An Introduction", in *Globalization, Growth and Sustainability*, edited by S. Gupta and N.K. Choudhry, pp. 1–13, Kluwer Academic Publishers, Springer, Boston, MA, https://doi.org/10.1007/978-1-4615-6203-0

Hammond, P. (1989). "Envy", in *The New Palgrave: Social Economics*, edited by J. Eatwell, M. Milgate and P. Newman, pp. 45–48, Macmillan, London

Hanushek, E.A., Schwerdt, G., Woessmann, L. and Zhang, L. (2017). "General Education, Vocational Education and Labour Market Outcomes Over the Lifecycle", *Journal of Human Resources*, 52(1), pp. 48–87

Harris, J. and Todaro, M. (1970). "Migration, Unemployment and Development: A Two-Sector Analysis", *The American Economic Review*, 60(1), pp. 126–142, www.jstor.org/stable/1807860

Hartman, R., Doane, M. and Woo, C.-K. (1991). "Consumer Rationality and the Status Quo", *Quarterly Journal of Economics*, 106(1), pp. 141–162

Heckman, J.J., Stixrud, J. and Urzua, S. (2006). "The Effects of Cognitive and Non-cognitive Abilities on Labor Market Outcomes and Social Behavior", *Journal of Labor Economics*, 24(3), pp. 411–482

Hirschman, A.O. (1958). *The Strategy of Economic Development*, Yale University Press, New Haven

IOM, International Organization for Migration (2020). *World Migration Report*, IOM, Geneve, wmr_2020.pdf (iom.int)

Ivanov, D. (2020). "Predicting the Impacts of Epidemic Outbreaks on Global Supply Chains: A Simulation-based Analysis on the Coronavirus Outbreak (COVID-19/SARS-CoV-2) Case", *Transportation Research*, part E, n. 136

Iyengar, S. (2011). *The Art of Choosing: The Decisions We Make Everyday – What They Say About Us and How We Can Improve Them*, Hachette Digital, London

Iyengar, S. and Lepper, M.R. (2000). "When Choice Is Demotivating: Can One Desire Too Much of a Good Thing?", *Journal of Personality and Social Psychology*, 79, pp. 995–1006

Johnson, E., Gachter, S. and Hermann, A. (2006). "Exploring the Nature of Loss Aversion. Institute for the Study of Labor", *IZA Discussion Papers*, www.researchgate.net/publication/5136284_Exploring_the_Nature_of_Loss_Aversion

Kahneman, D., Knetsch, J.L. and Thaler, R. (1990). "Experimental Tests of the Endowment Effect and the Coase Theorem", *Journal of Political Economy*, 98, pp. 1325–1348

Kahneman, D., Knetsch, J.L. and Thaler, R. (1991). "Anomalies: The Endowment Effect, Loss Aversion, and Status Quo Bias", *Journal of Economic Perspectives*, 5(1), pp. 193–206

Kahneman, D. and Snell, J. (1990). "Predicting Utility", in *Insights in Decision Making: A Tribute to Hillel J. Einhorn*, edited by R.M. Hogarth, pp. 295–310, University of Chicago Press, Chicago

Kahneman, D. and Snell, J. (1992). "Predicting a Changing Taste: Do People Know What They Will Like?", *Journal of Behavioral Decision Making*, 5(3), pp. 187–200

Kahneman, D. and Thaler, R. (2006). "Anomalies: Utility Maximization and Experienced Utility", *Journal of Economic Perspectives*, 20(1), pp. 221–234

Kahneman, D. and Tversky, A. (1979). "Prospect Theory: An Analysis of Decision Under Risk", *Econometrica*, 47, pp. 263–291

Katz, L. and Murphy, K. (1992). "Changes in Relative Wages, 1963–1987: Supply and Demand Factors", *The Quarterly Journal of Economics*, 107(1), pp. 35–78, www.jstor.org/stable/2118323

Keefer, P. and Knack, S. (2000). "Polarization, Politics, and Property Rights: Links between Inequality and Growth", *Policy Research Working Paper Series2418*, The World Bank

Knetsch, J. (1989). "The Endowment Effect and Evidence of Nonreversible Indifference Curves", *American Economic Review*, 79(5), pp. 1277–1284

Knetsch, J. and Sinden, J. (1984). "Willingness to Pay and Compensation Demanded: Experimental Evidence of an Unexpected Disparity in Measures of Value", *Quarterly Journal of Economics*, 99(3), pp. 507–521

Knight, F. (1933). "Memorandum on Banking Reform", March, Franklin D. Roosevelt Presidential Library, President's Personal File 431. K

Kolm, S.C. (1995). "The Economics of Social Sentiments: The Case of Envy", *The Japanese Economic Review*, 46(1), pp. 63–87

Komlos, J. (2014). "Has Creative Destruction Become More Destructive?", *CESifo Working Paper Series No. 4941*. https://www.cesifo.org/DocDL/cesifo1_wp4941.pdf

Krebs, T. (2007). "Job Displacement Risk and the Cost of Business Cycles", *American Economic Review*, 97(3), pp. 664–686

Krugman, P. (2009). "Increasing Returns in a Comparative Advantage World", mimeo, www.princeton.edu/~pkrugman/deardorff.pdf

Krugman, P. and Obstfeld, M. (1991). *International Economics*, Longman Higher Education, London

Krusell, P., Mukoyama, T., Sahin, A. and Smith, A. (2009). "Revisiting the Welfare Effects of Eliminating Business Cycles", *Review of Economic Dynamics*, 12, pp. 393–404

Krusell, P. and Smith, A. (1998). "Income and Wealth Heterogeneity in the Macroeconomy", *Journal of Political Economy*, 106, pp. 867–896

Kuznets, S. (1955). "Economic Growth and Income Inequality", *The American Economic Review*, 45(1), pp. 1–28, http://courses.nus.edu.sg/course/ecshua/eca5374/Economics%20growth%20and%20income%20inequality_Kuznets_AER55.pdf

Kuznets, S. (1963). "Quantitative Aspects of the Economic Growth of Nations: VIII. Distribution of Income by Size", *Economic Development and Cultural Change*, 11(2), Part 2, pp. 1–80

Lavoie, M. (1984). "The Endogenous Flow of Credit and the Post Keynesian Theory of Money", *Journal of Economic Issues*, 18(3), pp. 771–797, www.jstor.org/stable/4225471

Lazear, E.P. and Rosen, S. (1981). "Rank-Order Tournaments as Optimum Labor Contracts", *Journal of Political Economy*, 89(5), pp. 841–864

Le Clair, M. (2013). *Cartelization, Antitrust and Globalization in the US and Europe*, Routledge, London

Lindbeck, A. and Snower, D. (1984). "Involuntary Unemployment as an Insider-Outsider Dilemma", Seminar paper, Institute for International Economic Studies, University of Stockholm, No. 282, Stockholm

Liu, K., Salvanes, K. and Sorensen, E. (2012). "Good Skills in Bad Times: Cyclical Skill Mismatch and the Long-Term Effects of Graduating in a Recession", *NHH Dept. of Economics Discussion PaperNo. 16/2012*, https://ssrn.com/abstract=2135543 or http://doi.org/10.2139/ssrn.2135543

Lloyd-Ellis, H. and Bernhardt, D. (2000). "Enterprise, Inequality and Economic Development", *The Review of Economic Studies*, 67(1), pp. 147–168, www.jstor.org/stable/2567032

Lucas, R. (1987). *Models of Business Cycle*, Blackwell, Oxford

Lucas, R. (2003). "Macroeconomic Priorities", *American Economic Review*, 93(1), pp. 1–14

Lundberg, M. and Squire, L. (2003). "The Simultaneous Evolution of Growth and Inequality", *Economic Journal*, 113, pp. 326–344

Major, L. and Machin, M. (2019). "Social Mobility", *CEP, LSE, WPEA045*, November. https://cep.lse.ac.uk/pubs/download/cepcovid-19-004.pdf

Massey, D.S., Arango, J., Hugo, G., Kouaouci, A., Pellegrino, A. and Taylor, J. (1998). *Worlds in Motion: Understanding International Migration at the End of the Millennium*, Clarendon Press, Oxford

Mazzucato, M. (2013). *The Entrepreneurial State, Debunking Public vs. Private Sector Myths*, Penguin Books LTD, London

Milanovic, B. (2012). "Global Income Inequality by the Numbers: In History and Now – An Overview", *Policy Research Working Paper* 6259, The World Bank, Development Research Group, Poverty and Inequality Team, http://documents1.worldbank.org/curated/en/959251468176687085/pdf/wps6259.pdf

Milanovic, B. (2020). "After the Financial Crisis: The Evolution of the Global Income Distribution between 2008 and 2013", *MPRA Paper No. 101560*, https://mpra.ub.uni-muenchen.de/101560/

Miller, B. and Atkinson, R. (2013). "Are Robots Taking Our Jobs, or Making Them?", *The Information Technology & Innovation Foundation*, September, http://www2.itif.org/2013-are-robots-taking-jobs.pdf

Minsky, M. (1968). "Preface", in *Semantic Information Processing*, edited by M. Minsky, The MIT Press, Cambridge, MA

Mirrlees, J. (1971). "An Exploration in the Theory of Optimum Income Taxation", *Review of Economic Studies*, Wiley Blackwell, 38(114), April, pp. 175–208

Modigliani, F. and Brumberg, R. (1954). "Utility Analysis and the Consumption Function: An Interpretation of Cross-section Data", in *Post-Keynesian Economics*, edited by K. Kurihara, Rutgers University Press, New Brunswik

Mui, V. (1995). "The Economics of Envy", *Journal of Economic Behavior and Organization*, 26, pp. 311–336

Mukoyama, T. and Sahin, A. (2006). "Costs of Business Cycles for Unskilled Workers", *Journal of Monetary Economics*, 53, pp. 2179–2193

Mundell, R. (1957). "International Trade and Factor Mobility", *The American Economic Review*, 47(3), pp. 321–335, www.jstor.org/stable/1811242

Munoz, M. (2019). "How Much Are the Poor Losing from Tax Competition: The Welfare Effects of Fiscal Dumping in Europe", *WId Working Paper, n. 11.* https://hal-pjse.archives-ouvertes.fr/hal-02876988/document

Neisser, H. (1942). "Permanent' Technological Unemployment. Demand for Commodities Is Not Demand for Labour", *American Economic Review*, 32(1), pp. 50–71

Neutel, M. and Heshmati, A. (2006). "Globalisation, Inequality and Poverty Relationships: A Cross Country Evidence", *IZA Discussion Papers2223*, Institute of Labor Economics (IZA), http://ftp.iza.org/dp2223.pdf

Nordhaus, W. (1973). "Some Skeptical Thoughts on the Theory of Induced Innovation", *The Quarterly Journal of Economics*, 87(2), May, pp. 208–219

North, D.C. (1990). *Institutions, Institutional Change and Economic Performance*, CUP, Cambridge

Obstfeld, M. (1994). "Evaluating Risky Consumption Paths: The Role of Intertemporal Substitutability", *European Economic Review*, 38(7), pp. 1471–1486

Ocampo, J. (2015). "Capital Account Liberalization and Management", *Wider Working Paper, 2015/048.* https://www.wider.unu.edu/publication/capital-account-liberalization-and-management

OECD (1994). *OECD Employment Outlook*, OECD, Paris

OECD (1999). *OECD Employment Outlook*, OECD, Paris

OECD (2004). *OECD Employment Outlook*, OECD, Paris

OECD (2015). *Labour Shares in G20 Economies*, Report prepared for the G20 Employment Working Group, OECD, Paris

OECD (2018a). *A Broken Social Elevator? How to Promote Social Mobility. Overview of the Main Findings*, OECD, Paris, www.oecd.org/social/soc/Social-mobility-2018-Overview-MainFindings.pdf

OECD (2018b). *The OECD Risks that Matter Survey*, OECD, Paris, www.oecd.org/social/risks-that-matter.htm

OECD (2019). *Education at a Glance*, OECD, Paris, www.oecd-ilibrary.org/education/education-at-a-glance-2019_f8d7880d-en

Oreopoulos, P., von Wachter, T. and Heisz, A. (2012). "The Short- and Long-Term Career Effects of Graduating in a Recession", *American Economic Journal: Applied Economics*, 4(1), pp. 1–29

Oswald, A. (1986). "Unemployment Insurance and Labor Contracts Under Asymmetric Information: Theory and Facts", *American Economic Review*, LXXVI, pp. 365–377

Owyong, D. (2010). "Measuring the Trickle-down Effect: A Case Study on Singapore", *Applied Economics Letters*, 7(8), pp. 535–539, Published online: 05 Oct 2010, www.tandfonline.com/doi/pdf/10.1080/13504850050033337

Pagano, M. (1993). "Financial Markets and Growth: An Overview", *European Economic Review*, 37(2–3), April, pp. 613–622

Palley, T. (2001). "Endogeneous Money: What It Is and Why It Matters", *WP*, www.thomaspalley.com/docs/articles/macro_theory/endogenous_money.pdf

Papanikolaou, D. and Schmidt, L. (2020). "Working Remotely and the Supply-side Impact of COVID-19", *NBER Working Paper27330*, Cambridge, MA: National Bureau of Economic Research

Pemberton, J. (1996). "Growth Trends, Cyclical Fluctuations, and Welfare with Non-expected Utility Preferences", *Economic Letters*, 50(3), pp. 387–392

Persson, T. and Tabellini, G. (1991). "Is Inequality Harmful for Growth? Theory and Evidence", *NBER Working Paper3599*, National Bureau of Economic Research

Persson, T. and Tabellini, G. (1994). "Is Inequality Harmful for Growth?", *The American Economic Review*, 84(3), pp. 600–621, www.jstor.org/stable/2118070

Popper, K.R. (1935). "Logik der Forschung, Verlag von Julius Springer, Vienna", in *The Logic of Scientific Discovery*, Routledge Classics, London and New York, 2002

Rabin, M. (2002). "A Perspective on Psychology and Economics", *European Economic Review*, 46, pp. 657–685

Reinhart, C., Reinhart, V. and Rogoff, K. (2012). "Public Debt Overhangs: Advanced-Economy Episodes since 1800", *Journal of Economic Perspectives*, 26(3), pp. 69–86

Reinhart, C. and Rogoff, K. (2010). "Growth in a Time of Debt", *American Economic Review*, 100(2), pp. 573–578

Rodrik, D. (2000). "Growth Versus Poverty Reduction: A Hollow Debate", *Finance and Development*, International Monetary Fund, Washington, DC, 37(4), www.imf.org/external/pubs/ft/fandd/2000/12/rodrik.htm

Rodrik, D. (2004). "Industrial Policy for the Twenty-First Century", https://ssrn.com/abstract=617544 or http://dx.doi.org/10.2139/ssrn.617544

Rodrik, D. (2007). *One Economics Many Recipes: Globalization, Institutions and Economic Growth*, Princeton University Press, Princeton

Rodrik, D. (2016). "Premature Deindustrialization", *Journal of Economic Growth*, 21(1), pp. 1–33

Rodrik, D. (2018). "Populism and the Economics of Globalization", *Journal of International Business Policy*, 1(1–2), pp. 12–33

Roese, N.J. and Summerville, A. (2005). "What We Regret Most . . . and Why", *Personality and Social Psychology Bulletin*, 31, pp. 1273–1285

Root, B. and De Jong, G. (1991). "Family Migration in a Developing Country", *Population Studies*, 45(2), pp. 221–233, www.jstor.org/stable/2174780

Sachs, J., Benzell, S. and LaGarda, G. (2015). "Robots: Curse or Blessing? A Basic Framework", *Techn. Report21091*, National Bureau of Economic Research

Sachs, J. and Kotlikoff, L. (2012). "Smart Machines and Long-term Misery", *Techn. Report18629*, National Bureau of Economic Research

Salecl, R. (2010). *The Tyranny of Choice*, Profile Books Ltd, London

Salyer, K.D. (2007). "Macroeconomic Priorities and Crash States", *Economic Letters*, 94, pp. 64–70

Samuelson, P.A. (1948). "International Trade and Equalization of Factor Prices", *Economic Journal*, 58, pp. 163–184

Samuelson, W. and Zeckhauser, R. (1988). "Status Quo Bias in Decision Making", *Journal of Risk and Uncertainty*, 1(1), pp. 7–59

Santarelli, E. and Figini, P. (2002). "Does Globalization Reduce Poverty? Some Empirical Evidence for the Developing Countries", *Working Papers459*, Dipartimento Scienze Economiche, Universita' di Bologna

Scherer, F. (1979). "The Welfare Economics of Product Variety: An Application to the Ready-to- Eat Cereals Industry", *Journal of Industrial Economics*, 28(2), pp. 113–134

Schumpeter, J. (1976 first published 1943). *Capitalism, Socialism and Democracy*, Routledge, London and New York

Schwab, K. (2016). *The Fourth Industrial Revolution*, World Economic Forum, New York, NY

Schwartz, B. (2000). "Self-determination: The Tyranny of Freedom", *American Psychologist*, 55, pp. 79–88

Schwartz, B. (2004). *The Paradox of Choice: Why More Is Less*, Harper Perennial, New York

Schwartz, B., Ward, A., Monterosso, J., Lyubomirsky, S., White, K. and Lehman, D.R. (2002). "Maximizing Versus Satisficing: Happiness Is a Matter of Choice", *Journal of Personality and Social Psychology*, 83(5), pp. 1178–1197, https://doi.org/10.1037/0022-3514.83.5.1178

Scitovsky, T. (1992). *The Joyless Economy*, 2nd edn, Oxford University Press, Oxford

Sebastian, R. (2018). "Explaining Job Polarisation in Spain from a Task Perspective", *SERIEs: Journal of the Spanish Economic Association*, 9(2), pp. 215–248

Sennett, R. (1998). *The Corrosion of Character: The Personal Consequences of Work in the New Capitalism*, W.W. Norton, New York

Shapiro, C. and Stiglitz, J.E. (1984). "Equilibrium Unemployment as a Worker Discipline Device", *American Economic Review*, 74(3), pp. 433–344

Shaxson, N. (2019). "Tackling Tax Heavens", *Finance and Development*, September, IMF

Simmel, G. (1900). *Philosophie des Geldes*, Duncker &Humblot, Leipzig; *The Philosophy of Money*, Routledge, London and New York, 2004

Simon, H.A. (1947). *Administrative Behavior; A Study of Decision-making Processes in Administrative Organization*, Macmillan, Chicago, IL

Simons, H., et al. (1933). "Banking and Currency Reform", manuscript, printed in *Research in the History of Economic Thought and Methodology*, edited by Warren Samuels, Archival Supplement, Vol. 4, JAI Press, Greenwich, CT

Smith, A. (1776). *An Inquiry into the Nature and Causes of the Wealth of Nations*, The Modern Library, New York, 1937

Spitz-Oener, A. (2006). "Technical Change, Job Tasks, and Rising Educational Demands: Looking Outside the Wage Structure", *Journal of Labor Economics*, 24(2), pp. 235–270, https://doi.org/10.1086/499972

Stark, O. and Bloom, D. (1985). "The New Economics of Labor Migration", *The American Economic Review*, 75(2), pp. 173–178, www.jstor.org/stable/1805591

Stigler, G. (1971). "The Theory of Economic Regulation", *Bell Journal of Economics, The RAND Corporation*, 2(1), pp. 3–21, Spring

Stiglitz, J. and Fitoussi, J. (2009). "THE SHADOW GN*: The Ways Out of the Crisis and the Building of a More Cohesive World", in *The Ways Out of the Crisis and the Building of a More Cohesive World*, OFCE, Document de travail, N° 2009–17 Juillet 2009

Stiglitz, J. and Weiss, A. (1981). "Credit Rationing in Markets with Imperfect Information", *The American Economic Review*, 71(3), pp. 393–410

Tallarini, T. (2000). "Risk Sensitive Real Business Cycles", *Journal of Monetary Economics*, 45(3), pp. 507–532

Tinbergen, J. (1974). "Substitution of Graduate by Other Labor", *Kyklos*, 27(2), pp. 217–226

Todaro, M. (1976). "Migration and Economic Development: A Review of Theory, Evidence, Methodology and Research Priorities", *Occasional Paper 18*, Nairobi: Institute for Development Studies, University of Nairobi

Tönnies, F. (1887). *Gemeinschaft und Gesellschaft*, Verlag di Fues, Leipzig; *Community and Society*, Routledge, London and New York, 2017

Turner, A. (2013). "Debt, Money and Mephistopheles: How Do We Get Out of This Mess?", Speech, Cass Business School, https://webarchive.nationalarchives.gov.uk/20130403012143/www.fsa.gov.uk/static/pubs/speeches/0206-at.pdf

Turner, A. (2015). "The Case for Monetary Finance – An Essentially Political Issue", Paper presented at *the 16th Jacques Polak Annual Research Conference*, hosted by the International Monetary Fund, Washington, DC, November 5–6

Tversky, A. and Kahneman, D. (1991). "Loss Aversion in Riskless Choice: A Reference-Dependent Model", *Quarterly Journal of Economics*, 106(4), pp. 1039–1061

UNCTAD (2020). *World Investment Report*, https://unctad.org/system/files/official-document/wir2020_en.pdf

Veblen, T. (1899). *The Theory of the Leisure Class: An Economic Study of Institutions*, Unwin Books, London, 1970

Violante, G. (2008). "Skill-biased Technical Change", paper prepared for *the New Palgrave Dictionary of Economics*, www.econ.nyu.edu/user/violante/Books/sbtc_january16.pdf

Vivarelli, M. (2007). "Innovation and Employment: A Survey", *IZA Discussion PaperNo. 2621*, http://ftp.iza.org/dp2621.pdf

Vivarelli, M. (2014). "Innovation, Employment and Skills in Advanced and Developing Countries: A Survey of Economic Literature", *Journal of Economic Issues*, 48(1), pp. 123–154

Wang, P. (2008). "What Do You Mean by 'AI'?", *Frontiers in Artificial Intelligence and Applications*, 171(1), pp. 362–373, www.researchgate.net/publication/262357941_What_Do_You_Mean_by_AI

Wason, P.C. and Johnson-Laird, P.N. (1972). *Psychology of Reasoning: Structure and Content*, Harvard University Press, Cambridge, MA

WEF, World Economic Forum (2020). *The Global Social Mobility Report 2020, Equality, Opportunity and a New Economic Imperative*, World Economic Forum, http://www3.weforum.org/docs/Global_Social_Mobility_Report.pdf

Weiss, A. (1990). *Efficiency Wages: Models of Unemployment, Layoffs, and Wage Dispersion*, Princeton University Press, Princeton, NJ, https://doi.org/10.2307/j.ctt7zv0qf

West, D. (2015). "What Happens If Robots Take the Jobs? The Impact of Emerging Technologies on Employment and Public Policy", *Center for Technology Innovation at Brookings*, Washington, DC, www.brookings.edu/wp-content/uploads/2016/06/robotwork.pdf

Winkelmann, L. and Winkelmann, R. (1998). "Why Are Unemployed So Unhappy? Evidence from Panel Data", *Economica*, 65(257), pp. 1–15

Witt, U. (1996). "Innovations, Externalities and the Problem of Economic Progress", *Public Choice*, 89, pp. 113–130

Woodford, M. (2012). "Methods of Policy Accommodation at the Interest-Rate Lower Bound", Paper presented at *the Federal Reserve Bank of Kansas City Symposium on "The Changing Policy Landscape"*, Jackson Hole, Wyoming, August 31

World Bank (2019). *The Changing Nature of Work – World Development Report 2019*, Washington, DC: World Bank, http://documents1.worldbank.org/curated/en/816281518818814423/pdf/2019-WDR-Report.pdf

Wray, R. (2007). "Endogeneous Money: Structuralist and Horizontalist Approach", *The Levy Economics Institute, WP No. 512.* http://www.levyinstitute.org/pubs/wp_512.pdf

Wright, E. and Dwyer, R. (2003). "The Patterns of Job Expansions in the United States: A Comparison of the 1960s and 1990s", *Socio-Economic Review*, 1(3), pp. 289–325

Zingales, L. (2015). "Presidential Address: Does Finance Benefit Society?", *The Journal of Finance*, LXX(4), pp. 1327–1363

Index

Note: Page numbers in *italics* indicate a figure and page numbers in **bold** indicate a table on the corresponding page. Page numbers followed by "n" indicate a note.

Printed in the United States
by Baker & Taylor Publisher Services